What I Know About God

Library of Congress
_____TX 7-769-810 _____

Cover Artist: Catherine Courtlandt McElvane
Catherine-Courtlandt.com

Photography: Edison Searles
EdisonsPhotographics.com

Jewelry: Manetta Smith & Nina Kerr
beadsbybean.com

ISBN: 978-0-9829545-2-2

Frog's Hair Press
PO Box 34483
Charlotte, NC 28234

www.frogshairpress.com

frogshairpress@gmail.com

Printed in the United States
Revised October 2015

This is a work of fiction based on true events informing the spiritual understanding of a fictional character, Grace St.John. The characters of *What I Know About God* were first introduced in the novel, *Blood of Their Sons*.

INTRODUCTION

৵৵৵

This is not a book about religion; rather, an opportunity to hear a journey of self-discovery, hopefully without judgment, but with consideration of your own.

Each of us lives, loves, hopes. Each of us meets sadness, fear, and possibly regret during the course of our existence. Each of us is touched by the miracles that are life and death. In all these ways, we discover humanity. We discern rightness and wrongness, and group others based on their proximity to our understanding. In these ways, we find comfort in our sameness, and wallow in our differences. We judge and attach worthiness to others accordingly.

By virtue of our humanness, some question their place in the Universe, look for or to a God, or deny God's existence. In either event, we judge. This book asks you to suspend judgment-- of this book, yourself, of others. At the very least, imagine the idea.

Instead, consider this: For those who believe in a Creator of all things, there are as many paths to discover that Source as there are people present on the earth, people no longer in the physical, and people yet to be born. For those who do not believe in a deity, reflect upon the wisdom of Solomon: "All rivers run into the sea, yet the sea is not full". It applies here to suggest that in the macrocosm of thought, in the all-ness that is, there is room for all points of view, and more room still.

This is not a book about religion; it is a point of view about humanity, self-identity, and the personal convictions that inform the conscious recognition of both.

WHAT I KNOW ABOUT GOD
m.e.b.smith

Religion is for people who believe in hell.
Spirituality is for those who've been there.
— Native American quote.

I

In the Beginning...

My story begins in the novel, *Blood of Their Sons*. In it I describe an experience I had while in the hospital awaiting news about the fate of my daughter and first grandchild. Shannon had been shot and her unborn son was not expected to survive.

Both did survive, except the baby we welcomed into the world was not a boy. And, today, we celebrate Wren's tenth birthday.

After the most fantastic party any ten-year-old could wish for, thanks to me, my grandbaby took my hand and said, "Come on, Gaia, let's take a walk."

I knew the sound of that invitation. I had offered it many times after a vision, a visitor from beyond, or an insight I needed to share. We strolled down the path to the woods leading to Wren's playhouse. Her father had built her a nursery there that she named BeDa. Inside are some of the most exquisite flowers anyone could wish to see. All of her plants are poisonous; BeDa is short for beautiful death.

Wren is a miraculous young girl with mystic skills still unfolding. This little girl, at eight, was solving complex scientific problems. She was fascinated with the nature and properties of poisonous plants so we built her the nursery and a small laboratory. My first-cousin, Malice, is a forensic scientist and her mentor. Other parents would be leery to leave an eight-year-old with the occupants of her greenhouse; but, like I said, Wren is not *any* child.

Near the nursery is a dollhouse gazebo that I added to Wren's hideaway. A treasure chest held games that entertained us for hours as we drank tea and talked about everything. A natural stream trickled a few feet away. Pussy willow just starting to brown stood tall beside the water. Purple and white lilies, oleander and other poisonous plants dotted either side of the stream.

Sitting here reminded me of the day I sat with Wren's mother beside the water at a restaurant and told her about my journey through the Valley of Death, into the realm of Spirit, where our ascendants cross into the next existence. Wren sat in the baby seat and watched the water lap against the pier. On that journey I met The Mothers. They granted me time in the Temple of Tears, the Realm of Remembrance and the Sanctuary of Service. Though I was told of its existence, I did not travel the Road to Resurrection. I know it sounds ominous, but the boundaries beyond human existence are incomparable places of profound revelations.

Wren took my hand, interlocking our fingers. "Nice, right?"

"Very," I said. "No matter how many times I come here, it feels new every time. Something is always in bloom."

Silence rested between us until Wren said, "Tell me about God."

I'd love to say the question came from nowhere, but it didn't. Wren is a first-born female of a first-born female of generations of first-born women. That lineage bequeathed us with knowledge and capabilities that most people consider *special*. Today, Wren turned ten. Most ten-year-olds play computer games; Wren writes computer code to analyze the enzymatic properties of plants and their effect on humans. The way she explained it, enzymes are needed to break down chemicals. Plant-based enzymes become active as soon as they enter the body. Their effect is what interests her most. Ordinarily, her research would be considered mainstream, except for the fact that she was nine when she began.

It was inevitable that we would have this conversation. When she was younger, I told her about the journey I was granted the night she was born as if it were a bedtime story. She knew The Mothers had shared original knowledge, confirmed beliefs; had given me concepts to ponder and information to share.

"Gaia, don't leave anything out. I can take it, okay?"

Gaia is the name I insisted she call me. I would not be granny in this existence. At the time, I knew Gaia meant great mother. I learned through The Mothers that Gaia was an original deity who manifested as the Oracle of Delphi. She was *The* Mother of all the lesser gods. While that title was way bigger than I had the ego to wear, I would later learn that the title was appropriate; I am her descendent; she lives through the St.John women.

I took a deep breath and considered Wren's request as I observed this vibrant, beautiful little thing with the golden flecks in her green eyes, and silver hair framing her copper colored skin. She looked like a frosted gingersnap. Needless to say, this little Egyptian daughter attracted attention. She wore her shiny locks in a long ponytail like her mother had done for so many years. The style was easy and required no attention, leaving time to contemplate more important things – like quantum physics.

Wren has capabilities beyond me, beyond her mother. I knew she would understand whatever I shared with her to consider. But the comment actually meant she knew I would have to tell her about my life. It would be personal and complex, salty and sweet.

When she was seven, about the age as I when I had my first visit from the dead, Wren asked me about her grandfather, whom she had never seen. Her question centered on an event between my ex-husband and me that she had no way of knowing other than she knew. I'm sure she didn't know the specifics because the talent that

6

we share allows us some privacy from each other. I suspect she was reading some residual energy of his presence in my life.

So now, it was time to share memories. Something or someone had pointed her to this door inviting her to explore. But exploring her competencies meant opening myself to events that I had tucked away and hushed with a lullaby. That fact caused me a moment of unease. I wasn't sure how speaking the words would affect me after all these years, or what emotions would come with them. But it was my duty to help her, a vow I made to the Mothers and myself ten years ago.

"Well, the first thing you need to know is The Mothers call God FEWA-SUKU-BENSWA. They shorten it to SUKU which means Seen-Unseen-Known-Unknown."

"I know that much, Gaia, from your trip. FEWA means fire, earth, water, air. BENSWA is below, east, north, south, west, above." Wren hesitated. A grin tickled her cheeks. "Maybe that *trip* you took was courtesy of a plant."

"Oh no you didn't!" I shot back. After a deep breath I said, "Okay, I won't leave anything out."

II

All God's Children Got a Crown

"In African cultures, among others, it is believed a shaman, which is what you are my baby girl, must suffer in order to understand life. We all suffer. We may not all know love, but we all know suffering. It is the second great equalizer of life."

"What's the first, Gaia?" Wren asked.

"Death."

Many say that love conquers all. But being kissed by love does not save nor spare one from the duties and requirements of the human experience. In fact, the wise person is one who has known — or seen — great suffering and returned changed from its embrace. That change increases humanity, humility, knowledge of the oneness of life. It glimmers an awareness that there is something beyond our understanding.

Philosophers throughout time have spoken more eloquently than I dare try about the place suffering holds in our humanity. Even more, they talk about love. We all have experienced suffering, and most have experienced love in its various guises. We all have a badge of courage earned from our acquaintance with both. And yet, each of us unfolds differently.

There is so much mystery around how one becomes this or that, one kind of person or another. Two people born into the same family, community and background, with the same opportunities, can find themselves in different places socially, emotionally and spiritually. Why is that? What makes the difference?

The difference, my love, is how one responds to the invitations of life. Who we are can be found in how we journey *through* events. How we treat our physical being, how we evolve, how we transform. How we relate to other beings. How we forgive—or not; how we give or withhold, build or destroy.

So many of us deny responsibility with this universal excuse: 'I didn't have a choice'. What we're really saying is we surrendered to the circumstance. There was an honor to protect, a wrong to right, a deed to perform on behalf of the ego. We are always responsible for what we do, Wren. And yet, too many of us judge each other's unfolding, each other's choices as if we have been assigned that duty, but release ourselves from the same judgment.

It is my conclusion that God—the God that I know—cares very little about the loss or gain of something we deem important. God does not rate our life-changing events. God—the God that I know—is attentive only to the understanding we acquire from the experience. The first recognition is that nothing is ever lost. And

9

gain is not a reward. Not the thing from which we suffer, nor the love that we embrace.

Most people go through life looking for a prescription, a formula; some magic words that will grant their spiritual evolution, or their heart's desire, or affirm their standing with God. Some will tell you that whatever we do is pre-ordained, that we're puppets and God is working the strings. What I know is this: we come to who we are because of who we are.

"How do we know who we are?" Wren asked.

"Listen to your Spirit; it is the echo of what God whispered to you just before birth. God whispered to me: 'be kind, explore, help others remember'. The details are up to us in getting there.

"Some time ago I wrote a pre-bituary. In it, I described the kind of person I thought myself to be and the things I hoped to do by the time I die. As I matured, I made adjustments, but the vision of myself didn't change in any significant way. The core of who my spirit says I am is always there whether I act on it or not.

"Sweetness, we are the crown we grow into with each decision, each experience, each love; each loss. For me, the question is not how well I loved, or trusted, or lived, or treated others; or even suffered – but how much closer did I draw to my spiritual self, the crown I was presented, as a result of either."

III

Be Still and Know

"Gaia, tell me more about Spirit. There is more to it than doing or being a certain way, right? I mean, how do I know it's God speaking?"

"First, Spirit, with a capital "S", is the energy that connects us to God, who Native Americans call Great Spirit. This Spirit is not about doing, but being, so the question is how do we *feel, hear or see* God? The mechanism by which we communicate at every level is the Soul. It's our processing center and the communicator for Spirit. Within the Soul is a space called Higher Mind where we know without knowing. It doesn't need to learn or process; it is pure knowing and infinite possibilities. It is certainty without proof."

Before there were words to carry my awareness of God in gratitude upon the wind, I knew. When I looked upon the rituals of flowers that unfold in morning and preserve their beauty at night, I knew. I heard it in the clapping of the leaves upon trees that stood strong through every season. I felt it in the trickle of a stream playfully going where it was destined. It was in the strum of fishing wire I stretched around nails to make a guitar for your Aunt Lyn. The clack-clack-thump of the tin buckets your Uncle Dillon loved banging.

The cells within the cells of my body responded to the trees, the flowers, the birds, the drums — the sounds of life. I heard them all, saw the colors of their music and tried to paint them on canvas, but failed. Sometimes this awareness brought me to tears that flowed from a place I could not name or touch. These tears were neither of joy nor sadness, but tears of recognition, of synchronicity. There are no words to explain that feeling. Words are great at conveying intellectual ideas and thoughts, but not feelings and emotions. Words can be like glue that bind us or a sledgehammer that destroys. But tears are different; they can release from the Soul what words cannot.

Tears were the only way I could connect to the things around me: the ocean, mountains, rocks; everything. I was a child so I had no intellectual knowledge that this was true; I *felt* it to be so. More importantly, I did not manufacture this language; it was simply there. That awareness comes from Higher Mind. It is the state of being from which information flows without our involvement.

Along with my tears came a warming sensation. It was as if the sun had pinched a piece of itself and placed it in my chest. Once there, it warmed every ounce of me, and radiated outward. From that sensation came another: Silence. Words became meaningless. To utter anything would have defiled the moment.

You see, silence is a language too. It conveys far more deeply what words never will and what tears cannot. During a church sermon, I heard God's invitation to "Be Still and Know." At that moment, in the midst of religious clatter, I knew the voice of God.

Because of that invitation, I learned to hold my breath for long periods of time. God is between the breaths we take, between the blinking of our eyes, between the beats of our heart. In the grips of pain, or the turns of passion, our first thought is, *'Oh God'*. That's because God is between. Between here and there, right and wrong, courage and fear, life and death. God moves within: animating, radiating, blending; informing, transforming everything.

Get this: God told *Peace* to be still. Peace is already a state of calm, and to tell calm to be *still* -- wow! Take a minute and think about that!

Clearly, there is sacredness in silence. In silence, there is nothing— and everything. In stillness, we know who we are.

Spirit is the energy that connects us to God, and each other. It touches us in the arms of a lover, the kiss of a friend, the handshake of forgiveness; the embrace of reunion, the pat of a baby's hand on the face of its mother. In these moments, we know God.

Spirit whispers to us, guides us, silently beckons us to attune with Higher Mind. In response, the Soul answers.

IV

Life Connects with Life

"Wren, have you come across a concept called the Gaia Principle?"

"Come on, really?" Wren laughed.

"Trust me; I was as surprised they named it that as you are hearing it." But two scientists, a man named Lovelock—can you believe that—and a woman microbiologist, whose name is Lynn Margulis came up with it.

They hypothesized that organisms co-evolve with their environment; that they interact with their inorganic surroundings to form a complex, self-regulating, evolutionary system. Both: organisms and the environment, work together to maintain conditions that support life on Earth. One way they do this is by transferring information to each other."

"That makes sense to me. That says Earth is a progressive, living organism," Wren added.

"Imagine that! Yes, smarty pants, but the principle goes further."

"How do you mean?" she asked.

"I mean what Doctors Lovelock and Margulis postulated is absolutely true. The principle is the beginning of a deeper under-standing about connections between everything on the planet and is a peek at Higher Mind."

Growing up, I played with the ants and bugs that went about their business in the tall thickets near my grandmother's house. Grandma MaeAlice died not long after you were born. I wish you could have known her. She was some woman. But I'm sure she'll show herself to you at some point.

"You played with ants?" Wren teased.

I looked at her. "Who here plays with potted plants?" I lifted her arm in the air.

Anyway, those ants and bugs, would stop for a second, look up at me — wiggle their little antennas and return to their business. I watched birds build their nests and feed the mouths of barely chirping, thumb-size bodies with no feathers.

When a mother robin left one day, I reached into her nest and lifted a tiny blue egg in my hand. It was beautiful -- its bright color, the oval shape, the smoothness of this gift from its mother's womb. I returned the next day to that oak tree; much like that one over there, to find the egg had fallen from its nest and lay cracked on the ground. My heart ached as if I had lost something precious to me.

In tears, I carried the shell back home and made a nest from grass. I placed the broken egg in the nest and put that inside a yellow margarine container that I found in the trash.

I dug a small hole at the base of the tree with a spoon, and placed the handmade coffin inside. The mother robin flew from tree to tree, broadcasting her loss. She came low and watched as I covered the tiny grave and marked it with a cross I had made of twigs and black thread. We both sat quietly to honor the life that did not come forth; but yet, touched us deeply.

When I was older, I wondered if the mother had intentionally thrown the egg from the nest because I had touched it. Did she smell the scent of my hand and deemed the egg something that did not belong? We can change the course of history with the simplest, singular act.

How is it possible to affect and be affected by something that never took a breath? That was never even born? How are we capable of mourning the loss of something that never was? We mourn relationships that never existed. We miss people we've never met. Imagine that we are capable of affecting the course of a life without that life actually being present.

Within weeks of conceiving my first child, I called a friend to take me to the hospital. I was panicked; something was wrong. The doctor confirmed I had had a miscarriage. He touched my shoulder and said that I would be discharged when I was ready.

"You were pregnant before mom? I didn't know that."

I hesitated. Although I had promised to leave out nothing, I could not tell her the cause of my loss, that the sacrifice of my unborn child was the price of being a St.John. Nor could I tell her that she would one day do the same. Instead, I gently patted her hand in acceptance of her condolence. Her empathy was as warm as fresh bread.

Lying in the emergency room behind a thin green curtain, my friend held me as we wept in the silence of that little cubicle. The ripples of that green fabric separated life and death. On the other side of that thin faded curtain, people were doing, while behind their sight, we were being transmuted. Without words passing between to share our thoughts, my friend and I grieved the loss of laughter we would never hear, hugs that would not be felt; a date—that day—that would be forgotten in time.

On the ride home, I confessed. I blamed myself for the loss of my child because I had lifted a pail of water. I wasn't supposed to carry anything heavier than a laundry basket. Tears as heavy as that five-gallon bucket of water spilled out of me in grief that I could not contain.

17

Later, as I slept, induced by the sedative the doctor had given me, that robin's egg emerged in my dream. The pain in that memory wrapped itself around the pain of a new, similar loss, even in sleep.

My friend stayed all night, watching me surrender my grief to the depths of wherever that sedative had taken me. In my sleep I heard her pray to me, asking that I forgive myself. But in that place where I had gone, I held my child and knew that all was as it should be.

Morning came; my friend was asleep. I awoke to a sound outside the window. I rose from my bed and pulled back the curtain. Sitting on the limb of a tree branch about two feet away was a robin singing the most joyful bird song I might have ever heard. In the vibration of that song I felt these words: there is no loss, life connects with life, in every form, in every way; life connects with life.

V

We Are Guided by spirit

"What about spirit with a small s?" Wren asked.

"That's a sensible question. Let me tell you about Fire." It amazes me; it mesmerizes. All of the illnesses and injuries I have suffered are the result of fire. As a child, my tonsils were always inflamed. I have proof of burns on my feet, my arms, ears and buns. Mind you, I did not graciously accept when fire presented itself to me. But it was fire's way of bonding with me. I wear my scars as badges that say who I am — much like a name tag they stick on you at a conference that reads: "HI, My Name Is..." One scar even formed the likeness of a bird with no legs, with its head listening to the ground. "See," I said, showing her the scar. Perhaps it is the spirit of the tiny bird I planted at the base of that oak tree. The most clarifying moments of my life have been in the presence of fire that danced like a ballerina.

You've seen those charcoals in the grill as they're dying out, gray but still hot? Well, my temper is like that. Fire personifies my passion. If I could purify the hearts of people who take advantage of others, I would set them ablaze – figuratively speaking. I can't bear a lot of things: that commercial of the kitten with one eye. Child abuse. Words meant to harm for no reason other than to dominate or demean the listener. Anger feeds anger, and compassion gives birth to itself just as love gives birth to love. These are all small 's' spirits. You can feel these kinds of spirits just by walking into a room. Lots of religions recognize these as lesser gods.

One of the four elements chooses us before birth. Fire chose me. The fifth element accompanies each of them along with a secondary force.

"What is the fifth element?" Wren asked.

"It's called the Void. Some say the Void is emptiness. But the Void is a space of pure potentiality. It contains creativity, innate talent, intelligence, intuition, determination."

"Is the Void another word for Higher Mind?" Wren asked.

"Think of the Void as the state of consciousness to accept Higher Mind and the gateway to both is free will. For example: the 'idea' of something is in Higher Mind where it already exists. The Void holds the creativity and talent to bring the idea into the physical world. Free Will says it's your choice to do or don't do."

Through us, small 's' spirits experience the countless ways each can manifest its power. They don't take over us, but enliven our personalities. Some people are chosen by Earth. They are inspired by the land, mountains, trees, and countless other living things. Earth spirits are connectors. Reformers and restorers are of water, in all its guises. You find them in activism and nurturing others. Air informs and transports as in dance, music, architecture and literature. They create. Fire spirits transform.

Wren interrupted me. "Small "s" spirits are the same as Native Americans taking on the names of animals and such, right?"

Almost. Totems are used to show "kinship with" and are not limited to Native Americans. For example, the United States uses the donkey and the elephant to symbolize political ideals. Some states use animals or objects as symbols of their beliefs or legends.

Fire is a part of me; so is Air, my secondary force. I create and transform. Fire shows its power in the blood that warms us, in the passion that grows in a kiss from our beloved. Heat is necessary to grow our crops, prepare our food; comfort us from the cold. You know I love pottery and glasswork. To see something that was once clay transformed into objects of beauty through fire is mind blowing.

"No pun intended," Wren said.

"Of course it was; you know how I love words."

Anyway, when my time in this realm is over, I do not wish to transition through fire, mind you; but when I am done with the vessel that is my body, I want it to be consumed in flames. I want to be transformed in its grace back to that Orphic Spirit.

21

VI

Mother and Water – the Same

While I'm on the subject, let me tell you about one of the Mothers I met on my Journey. She rules over The Temple of Tears. She delivered this beautiful recitation and fed me something that looked like clear jellybeans as I listened.

"Gaia, did you know beans are considered the perfect food? They have lots of preventative and healing properties."

"No, I didn't know that. But I do love green beans, butter beans, snow peas, pinto beans, lima beans, sweet peas, lentils --"

" I get it, Gaia," Wren interrupted.

Anyway, with each *bean,* her presence intensified; I *felt* her words as if they were inside me. She told me why we cry. Tears of joy, tears of pain, they are the same. If we do not cry, that energy, that spirit, builds inside us. The energy must be released or it can cause great harm to our soul. Even now, I remember every word:

"My daughters brought you forth on the water's flow. She exclaimed in pain at the moment of your birth. You call her mother in honor of me. She wept in joy at the beauty of your being. Her lips turned to shape the moon. Look upon the Moon and see your Father's image shine upon me, pleased at your creation. Watch my face become full as he leaves to make provisions for his children and return again to me.

I gave your mother the sound she made at your birth because it is my sound. She gave this sound to you so that you might call upon her in your distress. You call her name, in my name, so that I might be with you. I taught your mothers to cry with you and for you. I taught her to give me her tears so that our bond would always be. For time upon time your mothers kept our bond. With our tears we gave life and sustained you.

I come now to share my grief. You must hear the sound I made at your birth and remember it. See my tears. They are water. They renew. Look at how I w ash the earth with my tears. From my tears -- you are. I gave your mother my sound and my Being to remember her bond with me. Each month she fills with water as a reminder of our bond. Each month she cries my tears without knowledge because she has forgotten. Against the natural order, some of my daughters stopped their tears and broke our bond. I have come to share my tears -- not in joy but in sorrow.

I worry about your children. I worry about my daughters who abuse them. Some nurse their seeds in toxic wombs of grief and shame; despair and anger. I worry because you do not cry for them. I mourn because you have not given them my sound. Your children make their own sound and you do not hear them. In your distress you curse their name.

I have come to remind you... to bring you to my breast so that you might feel my heart. See how my body rises. See the tears I have for you. See and feel my sorrow and my joy. My daughters: give me your tears.

My sons: honor your mothers as they are of me. Smile upon them as your Father smiles upon me. When you look upon the sun with its face upon the moon, know this. Hear my sound in my daughters' cry and in the distress of your children. Open your arms to them. Let their tears fill the valley of your necks. Be the ocean into which they cry. Let their tears wash upon you as my tears flow upon your Father.

My obedient daughters ask what they can do to make life heaven on earth. I say to them – Be of me."

Ashe.

VII

There are Unspoken Agreements

Like most of the families in my neighborhood, mine was poor. Alongside most of with them, I worked for Mr. Cooley, picking cucumbers, peas and strawberries in the summer and cotton in the fall. I missed the first month of school every year from the time I could bend and pull until I was twelve years old. Some kids became adults in those fields. I can still see them with their hand out to Mr. Cooley on Friday. I can't remember how much we were paid, but it was just above free labor.

I was so thin I barely cast a shadow. A person like me had to work long and steady to net a hundred pounds of the South's white treasure. It took all day -- from the time the sun first peaked through darkness until there was just enough evening left for supper. The senior pickers, older women, mostly, could do three and four hundred pounds before the first bead of sweat.

The cotton was so closely planted each row looked like a mile of braided white knots with green accents where leaves still clung to the stalks.

Cotton sacks were about four feet long and three feet wide. Each was custom-fitted to the owner so that it hung across the

25

shoulder just the right length to allow the hand to flow easily into the sack and out again. Different colored straps helped tell which sack was whose. Sometimes we carried our sacks home at the end of the day as a carpenter would his tools. Sometimes we left them on the back of the pick-up truck that dropped us off in the evening and picked us up at daybreak.

The senior pickers were so good they blocked off ten rows at a time. Children picked on the same rows as their parents or took the ones right beside their mothers so they could be trained in the art of picking cotton, and simultaneously kept out of mischief. Children had a tendency to wander the rows, throwing the hard, unopened boles that sometimes hit the wrong person. So they were kept under the mother's stern voice and the reach of her spanking hand should that be required.

Every child had a job in the field. The littlest kids carried a mason jar filled with ice water from person to person — most of whom had a collapsible metal cup tied to the sack. Some pickers drank if they were thirsty; some wet the bandana tied around their head or drenched their frayed straw hats.

When another handful of cotton could not find room, the sack was propped in the middle of the row. The older children made a game of dragging the packed sacks to the pickers' sheets. It would take two or three of them to pull it, the racers tripping and falling several times along the way.

The cotton field was my first classroom in Agreements. The ladies of the field supervised the rest of us. Although there was no one in charge, this was their workplace and they said how, when and what took place. There were scheduled rest breaks and lunch time was like a picnic. We brought coolers packed with fried chicken, fresh tomatoes, potato salad and lemonade with the squeezed lemons floating in the jar. If we wanted a hot meal, we'd simply set tin pans of food wrapped in foil in the sun an hour before noon.

No one blew a whistle or rang a bell. When the self-imposed leader did anything, the others followed. If she happened to stretch longer than usual, the rest of us responded to this as a break. She'd correct our error with laughter and instruct us to keep going. "Not yet," she'd yell. "Not yet. Let's get another row."

The experienced pickers draped several sacks around their neck at once. They were long enough to double as a twin-size mattress, and often did -- placed under the tall stalks for the little ones when they got sleepy.

I learned the value of proper breathing in that field: the steady, even inhaling/ exhaling that enabled these experts to master two hundred pounds of cotton by noon.

I learned to grab and release from another. None was concerned with pulling the white fleece neatly from its bole where some of it stuck like clam meat. Instead, they'd grab shell and all. This was not the desire of the cotton owner, mind you. For one thing, the boles added weight to the scale. It was also extra work for the machine to sort out this non-usable byproduct. So, Mr. Cooley ended up paying for something he couldn't use and stressing the machine to do something it wasn't designed to do.

Miss Lizzie told the kids, "Pee on the cotton" when we had to go. Cotton held water a long time. One of the reasons the elders pushed themselves in the morning was because the cotton was wet with dew. So, they rushed to fill their sacks before the sun sat high in the sky. Once packed until it bulged, the sacks with damp cotton were put in a shady place for later. These were emptied in the middle of the sheet between dry cotton at the end of the day before the sheets got weighed. Dark brown spots were visible in the bales from those who dipped snuff or chewed tobacco. Every ounce of moisture mattered. The men bet each other a drink of Grandma Alice's moonshine on whose sheet would weigh the most.

I found the courage to ask if these practices were fair.

"No, baby, it ain't fair," Ms. Lizzie said. "But it's the way it's done. Ya see, Mr. Cooley and us have this agreement that ain't wrote down nowhere. He pays us less than what we's due and we do whatever we can to make up the diff'rence."

She made it personal. "Didn't your grandma tell me you need a new pair'a shoes for school this year?"

"Yes'm," I said.

"Uh-huh," she acknowledged. "Well, how long you think it take you to earn enough to buy them shoes and paper and stuff you gon' need if you picked this here cotton to suit Mr. Cooley, when he thinks you's just fine barefoot?"

No more words passed between us that day. At quitting time, when the truck came and Mr. Cooley weighed our work for the day, I had picked my first hundred pounds of cotton—one hundred and fifteen pounds to be exact. My teacher looked at me, turned away from the clearing, tilted her head, and gave a confirming spit of warm brown juice.

Wren was silent for several seconds before she said, "That's a good story, Gaia, but I don't get it."

Well, baby, we act upon unspoken agreements all the time. People have unspoken agreements about racism, women act in agreement with sexism. In fact, women subvert our role as the keepers of civilization by trading our voice and our power for perceived security. Men act in agreement with paternalism and

29

misogyny out of the notion that they have dominion. Sadly, they approach women out of resentment or fear-- not reverence.

Likewise, we have Unspoken Agreements with God. These are often called Spiritual Laws. I prefer Unspoken Agreements. To agree means to act in harmony with another — with the environment, society, with your own character; with God. The ladies and Mr. Cooley allowed, accepted; acted in harmony with the behavior of the other even though on the surface, it appeared they were taking advantage of each other.

If you know your environment you can choose to act upon it in agreement. Unaware, we get acted upon. We criticize, we play victim -- like dust on a broom. When life is hard, we think God is punishing us out of this ignorance. During the time we picked cotton, society denied black people the most basic rights and granted little more than a teaspoon of humanity. The workers knew the limitations imposed upon them and Mr. Cooley understood his advantage. So, they had this unspoken agreement and acted in alignment with it.

The truth is: Truth is temporary. What we learn replaces what we know. We collaborate with God and each other to create and manifest at our level of awareness. We act in Agreement always at the level of our understanding and acceptance.

As we grow in Awareness, we increase our vibrations, our humanity with one another and our connection to God. We come to understand that our relationships have value far beyond what is obvious and present. We recognize that every person has a role in expanding The Creation. Through Awareness, we better access and impart knowledge, wisdom and our talents. God Intends that we live in this awakened state of being. That we tap into Higher Mind and utilize the Void. When we do, truth changes.

"The Creation of what, Gaia?" Wren asked.

"I don't have a clue, sweetheart." I answered. "There is a humongous cosmic event going on in which each of us has a starring role, but the ending is a mystery - at least to me."

Simply put, the Unspoken Agreement is that God will not judge us as we grow in consciousness. And we agree to grow into our crown -- even as we take advantage and get taken; even as life seems unfair, even as we think God should intervene. Even as we screw up our part of the agenda, the event goes on perfectly.

"So, like you old folk say, 'it's all good,'" Wren said.

"Yep. ...except for that old folk comment, young lady. I am not in agreement with that."

"Sorry, Gaia, the spirit of teasing got me."

"Uh-huh."

VIII

A Purpose Can Seem Small, but Is No Less Than the Prophets'

"Well, what do you know, that story was a great segue to talk about relationships," I said.

"Okay, I'm ready," Wren said and shifted for comfort.

I want you to know about Mr. Cecil Whitman. He was brilliant, and he was a drunk. He was a carpenter by trade, a fact not lost on me when I learned about another alleged carpenter named Jesus. It would be three decades later before I would fully understand and appreciate the depth of Mr. Cecil's role in my life. It seems he existed solely for me. His purpose was to gently blow his breath upon the embers of my soul, igniting my desire for knowledge. This man taught me, beyond his death, that there are no small deeds; that all God's children got a crown.

When he had a job to do, he didn't drink. That was his work ethic. He would say, "Never do something the wrong way three times when you can do it right only once." He said, "The quality of your work speaks to the kind of person you are." I hold that work creed to this day. He loved making crooked shelves straight again, or caulking and framing windows to keep out the cold. He made lumpy floors flat; he built cabinets and hung doors and windows. He was a master of his craft -- when he was sober.

He was never sloppy drunk, but went into such a stupor he seemed to leave his body. He sat upright; head bowed, arms across his chest, legs crossed at the knee, and mumbled some ancient language. I concluded that he drank to connect with whatever gods met him in that space between his reality and theirs. When he returned, he spoke as if given special instructions he had to share, whether or not anyone listened.

Sitting under the collection of shade trees in the front yard of my grandmother's house, he'd recite the gods' messages to me. I spent countless summer days in his company, hearing his stories. I don't know when, how or why I became the repository of his knowledge, but I felt chosen.

One day he said to me, "You're special, little one." Another man would say those very words to me three years later. Mr. Cecil held my tiny hands in his and smiled at me. I was seven, I think. From that time on I became his student.

I had first and second grade teachers by now, but Mr. Cecil out ranked them all. He showed me that books are about more than reading. Through the magic of words, I left the cruelty of our existence and traveled the world. I met Aladdin and powerful genies. I sailed with Jason and the Argonauts to find a golden fleece. I followed Poseidon through the seven seas, befriended

Thor, whose hammer made the lightning, and watched Aphrodite's arrows purify hearts with love. Prometheus brought fire to the people but was bound to a rock; vultures picked at his eyes and ate his liver for a hundred years. He is a reminder that progress comes at a price; that no good deed goes unpunished.

Mr. Cecil taught me to find the big dipper in the sky and to wonder at the power of the moon. His wisdom helped me to look beyond what my eyes could see and find a deeper vision.

This was especially true when it came to African-Americans' role in advancing civilization. He told me a black man, Garrett Morgan invented the streetlight, John Albert Blair invented the rotary lawn mover, and Dr. Charles Drew pioneered blood transfusions. Did you know that Dr. Patricia Era Bath, a woman of our time, invented laser eye surgery and holds four medical patents! The textbooks from which we were taught had none of that. What we knew about black history amounted to stories of slavery and despair, and how a white man granted freedom that wasn't free, nor his to give. Our payment for the Gettysburg Address came in daily installments. Some days, the payment was humiliation. Others got invoiced payable in death -- they were lynched, severely beaten, or burned alive. Even today, a bill comes due in somebody's mailbox, and we're still paying interest.

"Mr. Cecil sounds nice, " Wren said. What was he like?"

"Oh, my goodness," I chuckled. Mr. Cecil was five-feet-six with wavy hair the color of black patent leather shoes. Short, compared to most other men, he told me to look everyone in the eye when I spoke. He said the ground cannot see into my heart so why ask it to try. He said to never hold anyone above or place anyone beneath me. To recognize that every living thing has value and purpose. My tutor's life and our relationship lived that wisdom. I was a child and my purpose was to be his friend. He was a carpenter who helped to build my life.

I can see his face; the color of honey. His whole family had the same complexion. It was said his grandfather was pure Indian. I suspect both his parents had Indian blood. The whole family had straight, black hair and shined like toasted peanuts.

He always wore a baseball cap and flannel shirts, with khaki pants. He stepped lightly in his loafers, almost on tiptoe, as if afraid he'd crush the littlest thing beneath his feet. He wobbled a little when sober but never when drunk. It was as if someone else used his body and the alcoholic wobble waited until he was back in possession of his limbs.

"He sounds kinda geeky," Wren said, smiling. "What else?"

Well, he had a sense of humor and a light, even-toned voice that produced short, mumbled laughter when he found something funny. He smiled most of the time and was pleasant to everyone, tipping his cap to any woman nearby. Mr. Cecil never married; he lived with his mother and father for all the years I knew him.

I remember asking him, "What should I be when I grow up?"

He shifted this short stubby cigar that sat between his lips like a permanent accessory. He flicked his lighter at the tightly wound brown stump with the paper band still intact. I held my breath thinking he would light his thick moustache if he ever succeeded in setting the cigar afire. He took a few quick puffs and said, "Be what God put in you to be."

"But my teacher said I can be whatever I want to be."

"Well, can you be a giraffe?"

I giggled at the thought. "No," I said.

"What your teacher meant is that one day people, even black people will be able to express themselves with pride; without limitations on who God intended we be. Some day a black man will be president of these United States because God will ask him to lead."

"Well, what about me?"

"No, God didn't make you to be president."

He was teasing, I knew. But I also knew he was telling me that each of us is meant for something special to each of us.

"You should be president," I told him. He smiled weakly and lowered his eyes, giving his gaze to the earth below.

I got a music box for Christmas that year. When I opened the lid, a pink little girl in a pink crinoline skirt with colored sparkles, popped up. The music played and she softly twirled on her pedestal. Music and dance, that day, became a part of me. I wanted to be a ballerina. Hidden in the woods near grandmother's house, I would bend my wrists above my head and swirl on tiptoes until I became too dizzy to stand. The whole Earth spun -- the trees and the sky -- as I lay on my back where I fell. I couldn't tell if I was still swirling or the world had become a part of my dance. Once the sensation passed, I'd do it again and again, until I became too drunk to move. Even now, I love dancing.

Later in life I came to realize that any parent or teacher who tells a child he or she can be anything they want to be is doing the child possible harm. Instead, listen to the child. Early on, we know what we're here to do. We should honor what God placed in each heart, and nurture it. That doesn't mean God only gave us one 'to do'; we could have a grocery list of to do's. Nor does it mean that we can't explore other things along the way—all knowledge is useful and helps us to discover who we are; and are not. God would not give you a purpose that is not a part of the greater story, that does not advance evolution. Exploration is half the fun!

"There are people doing the same thing. Do they have the same purpose?" Wren asked.

The possessions for expressing a purpose are unique to each person. Even if the purpose seems to be the same thing someone else is doing, only you can do you; how you express you is proprietary; you own the trademark. I've had many teachers, but every one of them was different, each imparted knowledge in their own way. Every musician makes music with his and her own sound.

Getting that music box, being introduced to dance, was a gift. Dancing connected me to Spirit and allowed it to speak in a language that opened a portal to my soul. It showed me something about who I am. It added dimension to my life and gave me an outlet for my sadness more times than I can say. It still moves me beyond my circumstance, and invites me to twirl in joy.

Wren, when we honor the blessing of our possessions, when we listen to what God whispered to us to be, when we perform our work the very best we can, we move the world towards perfection.

IX

What God Will Do Is Already Done

Growing up I always felt out of place, like I was born in a place I didn't belong. This feeling out of place had some to do with my family; they all seemed to fit together. But in a family of brown ducks, I was a green chicken.

"I know what that's like," Wren said.

"Yes, you do," I smiled. Even more, the feeling had to do with where I grew up. I loved the country, mind you; still do. There is nothing like the feel of warm powdered dirt between your toes in summer. Or the smell of summer rain. Chasing fireflies at nightfall and junebugs during the day. Imagine the hard pounding of a thunderstorm on a tin roof. You have not tasted fresh unless you've picked a tomato from the vine, dashed it with salt and felt the drizzle of lukewarm juice down your chin. I loved every minute of growing up a country girl. But there was always a mustard seed of something inside me waiting for the soil it needed to grow.

So I daydreamed a lot about where I must have been meant to be. I read about places that could have been my home: Egypt or Greece, Rome or France. Perhaps my roots were meant for one of those places with vast ancient histories and grand mythic tales. I lost myself in stories about Zeus, Diana and Loki. The legend of the gods, like Atlas holding the world on his shoulders, nourished me. I comforted myself with fairytales of *Sleeping Beauty* and *Rapunzel*. I tossed at windmills with Don Quixote and conquered the seas with Sinbad. Books became my friend and refuge. Through them I searched for home. Though them I met others like me: misfits. Like them, I imagined some epic journey that was mine to take in search of myself; to return home again, whole.

I had not heard the word college until I was eleven. It came from the mouth of an unlikely messenger: Mr. Cecil. And yet, it wasn't unlikely at all. He was the smartest man I knew. He was a shy misfit like me. He too was in a place he didn't belong. The shackles of Jim Crow held him tightly to the bosom of the dirt that caught him when he fell.

And so we sat beneath the big oak tree on the edge of my grandmother's land and looked across the sky, hoping to see something recognizable in the clouds that would point the way. Beneath the broad leaves of the white oak tree, he told me about the universe and the wondrous depths of space. We talked about energy and gravity and death. With the ridges of that tree pressed against our backs while we watched ants trail across its massive roots, he made me promise I would go to college.

"What's college?" I asked.

"It's freedom," he said.

I had wonderful teachers throughout my school years. There is not one who looked into my face and did not see the promise Mr. Cecil made me swear. I didn't speak of it to them; it's as if they saw what he saw, knew what he knew: that I belonged some place else. Each must have made a private vow to help fulfill that promise. The word 'college' sprang from their mouths for the whole class to hear, but I knew it was meant for me.

Even before them, my mother forced my feet onto the road of this unknown journey. Yes, forced. My child-mind at the time did not understand why she turned into this crazed woman threatening my brutal death if I did not learn. I was five when I went to first grade. My birthday came after the cutoff to register so she changed my date of birth to ten days earlier.

The first weeks of school were spent learning the alphabet and numbers. We learned their sounds and practiced making those letters on unbleached paper that looked like it had been pounded into sheets straight from the tree. I quickly learned to trace the letters already inked on the light blue lines and then duplicate rows of that letter on my own with ease.

Weeks later, our first grade teacher, Ms. Sparks, gave us our very own book. It was a used paperback of a little boy and girl with pink skin and cherry cheeks. On the cover with them was a black dog named Spot. The book told us the one-sentence adventures of Dick and Jane. One day I had had enough of Dick and Jane and Spot. The homework Ms. Sparks had assigned sat on the floor where I dropped it. Off I went to chase chickens. I wasn't gone long when mama called me in a raised voice, "Come here, gal!"

Dutifully, I went, unaware I had made an egregious mistake. When I got within arm's reach, she snatched me up with one hand and started slapping my behind with the other. My little legs looked like dueling chopsticks. She then plopped me in a wooden chair.

"What is this?" She yells.

"Through grape size tears I saw that she was holding Dick and Jane. I looked at her puzzled.

"What is it?!" She repeated.

I managed what was clearly an obvious answer.

"And what is this?" She said, holding up Ms. Sparks' assignment.

"My homework," I sobbed. Those gumballs of water streaked the dust I had collected from running down chickens.

"Don't you ever come home and not do your homework; you hear me!"

And so began my commitment to fulfill a promise unspoken for five more years. I don't think college for me was her motivation, but it was as if mama knew I would one day get there. And in the only way she knew how, she was preparing me to leave the place she called home.

As I grew older, I became aware of the reality that must have sat on Mr. Cecil's front porch and bullied him year after year until the only way to befriend it was to drink: we were black and poor. My whole community was black and poor. That was our reality. The only dream we dared to have was getting a good job at one of the nearby factories, finding someone to marry and creating a new batch of disillusioned. I wanted none of either. All the same, I felt a disappointing truth in my soul; it shifted something in me: college cost money, and we had none to spare.

I became angry with my teachers who dangled the word before me like a ticket to Everywhere. I had to swallow my heat. They were dealing with strife and uncertainty that came to their door, too. It was the sixties and our high school was being dismantled, bussed away and integrated into a culture that did not want us.

That experience marked progress for me in one instance and conflicted me in another. Integration changed my life, period. It shattered the hard familiarity of my existence and replaced it with volcanic turmoil that cultivated massive evolutions. I was in its wake. Stripped; yet suckled, tossed overboard into raging waters that flowed to a calmer sea.

Meanwhile, I took a seat in this new reality and resigned myself to time. I turned to books and school. I would continue to leave the town with no traffic light for the sands of Arabia and the safaris of Africa. I would worry about finding one of those good jobs at the factory when summer school was over. For now, I dreamed the dreams of Mr. Cecil and all the teachers who saw past my present.

Here is where my promise began to germinate. My mother had taken one of a few jobs I'd ever known her to have. For the summer, she assisted a white teacher at the elementary school. My summer school English teacher was also white. One day, she asked, as if she knew of my promise, "Where are you going to college?"

The slow response burned in my throat. "I'm not going."

"What? Oh, my goodness," she said. "You must!"

To satisfy her, I told her I'd thought about going to the Air Force; that I would go to college through the military.

"But there's a war! What did your mother say about that?"

"We haven't talked about it yet."

She obviously saw the shame in my face and changed the subject by giving me something to do to help her close out the day.

Two days later, my mother asked me to come to the elementary school after class. There, she introduced me to the teacher for whom she worked. "Mrs. Stewart wants to meet you. Her daughter is your teacher," she said.

I had not known that; there was no reason I should. Ms. Stewart reached out her hand. "My daughter is taken with you, young lady. Ms. Nola, she tells me this bright young thing isn't going to college?"

"We can't afford it, right now," Mama said. "Maybe I'll be able to save enough to get her in next year." We both knew that was a lie. The only thing we had left over after paying bills was more bills.

Ms. Stewart reached for a manila envelop on her desk and handed it to me. She smiled. "Fill this out and get it back to me tomorrow first thing."

I began reading. It was an application to St. Andrew's Presbyterian College. "But it says registration ended two weeks ago."

Mama added her reminder, "We can't afford it, Ms. Stewart. I wish I could send her, but I can't. I'm hoping she'll get a job at the Fieldcrest Plant to help with the family. She's so smart, they might let her work in the office." I hated my mom at that moment for saying that, and for the circumstance of our existence.

Ms. Stewart looked at me and smiled. "Get it done, and your mother will bring this back to me tomorrow; can you do that?" I nodded in response, looking at my mother for approval.

The following week, an envelope arrived from St. Andrew's Presbyterian College. The package contained a map of the campus with the dormitory locations and my assignment. I literally trembled. I grabbed my bike and peddled down the back road to the elementary school to question Mrs. Stewart, the mother.

"Your mama is a sweet woman," she said. "And my daughter talks about you everyday. When she learned you weren't go to college, she made me do something about it. I'm on the Board at St. Andrew's and I called in a favor. Everything is paid for, darling. You go make us proud. But only if your mama says you can."

I didn't know it at the time, but Mama knew my frustration better than I gave her credit. That day was the only time I'd ever seen my mother cry tears for me. They flowed across her face in stoic calm. She looked at Ms. Stewart and said, "Of course she can make us proud. She does it everyday."

I had no idea she felt that way. In that moment, my heart warmed towards my mother for the first time in the six years since she'd come home from New York and collected Lyn, Dillon and me from Grandma Alice. Pools of water glossed my eyes both from appreciation of the words she'd just spoken, and fear she didn't mean them. She had never shown or said anything complimentary of me til now. The night I had taken the application home, I had heard my stepfather tell her I didn't need college; that the factory was hiring and I needed to get a job. More often than not, she listened to him and did what he wanted, especially regarding the children who were not his blood.

I looked at her with eyes that portrayed years of what it meant to be a green chicken in her brown duck family. I got on my knees and laid my head in my mother's lap. I looked up. Images of Mr. Cecil rested in my eyes embraced in the fear that what broke him would find me.

My mother looked down at me and said, "This is God's work, child; nobody but God. It was already done."

X
Cruelty is Man-Made

The hardest thing for me to accept is that I choose the circumstances of my life. For the most part, I choose. Without question there are those I had to navigate not of my making. Some will tell you we choose them all. I disagree. We often find ourselves in the wake of someone else's choices. But more than not, the events of my life were shaped by my decisions, my actions and inactions.

I grew up hearing that God controls every detail: from our rising in the morning to our sleeping at night. From the cooling rain, to the bloom on the morning glory. If I was in turmoil, God put me there to teach me a lesson. Whatever I didn't get wasn't meant for me. Every good and bad thing that ever happened to me was God's will. In my soul I didn't feel these claims to be true, but it was convenient to put the responsibility on Fate and accept whatever was happening as beyond my control.

Needless to say, we lacked a lot of luxuries so I was happy when God found me worthy of new shoes or blessed me with a tough cut of beef to replace the chickens we plucked and ate on a regular basis.

I sank into depression when the job I prayed for to take me out of my circumstance went to someone else. People appeased me by saying: "God has something better for you." How could God not want me to make more money to better provide for my family? I could not reconcile ministers preaching I had not because I wanted not, with the fact that I wanted a life I wasn't getting.

So, without contradictory evidence to support my disbelief, I accepted that God was withholding from me and went about life with the knowledge that I had no choice; that tribulation was standard issue and everybody got some assigned at birth. Whatever sin I committed had not been washed away in baptism. That was my logic when my husband hit me for the tenth time. Even as I accepted my situation, I resisted. If I had to go through, it would get no cooperation from me.

I fought back by continuing to educate myself however I could. I would not be dependent on someone else for the state of my existence. Still, I rationalized my choice of this husband by focusing on the truth that he was a loving, attentive father at the time. That was his value to me. All the same, I wish that I had chosen differently for your mother's sake. She loved her dad; it would have been good for both if she could have shown him so.

"How did you two meet, Gaia?" Wren asked.

49

Your grandfather and I met in college. I had never really dated before he came along. I only had one boy friend in high school who came to my grandmother's house to see me. We sat outside and talked, or walked the narrow dirt road to town for a popsicle and back. I had never been *out* on a date. I was going to college on a promise to make people proud, to go find my place in the world. So, truth be told, I was as dumb as a hole in the road when it came to boys.

At St. Andrews, a sport activity was required of all freshmen. I want to say swimming was that sport because I can't imagine taking it otherwise. I lived in the country. The nearest recreational water was Jones Lake, a spot where Blacks could go and enjoy the semblance of a beach. It was fifty miles from where we lived. I don't know if Jones Lake was man-made, or its size; I vaguely remember going there. The only other swimming place was this stretch of a hole in the ground that collected water and turned green. Some of the boys were brave, or stupid, enough to jump into it. Why boys do what they do remains a mystery to me.

I had also been a sickly child. Fire showed up as tonsillitis. The fever and infections damaged my eardrums. My grandmother stuffed cotton in my ears a lot because they sometimes leaked a yellowish-green ooze.

"Ewww," Wren grimaced.

"And it smelled worse!" I teased her. I used cotton balls to keep water from getting in even when I took a bath. I always imagined it was some of the cotton I'd picked for Mr. Cooley as a child. The doctor had said I could become disoriented if water got into my ears. I figured that meant I'd start turning around like a dog chasing its tail then bump into a tree. Nonetheless, I took swimming. I somehow managed to get money for a swimming cap and the college provided earplugs.

"Gaia, are you going to tell me how you met grandfather?"

"Yes, Miss Thank You Ma'am. I'm getting to that. Now, where was I? Oh yes, swimming."

Like many times before, my mother had gotten a box of hand-me-down clothes from somewhere. This stuff had to have come from a white family because I didn't know any black people who owned the kinds of things she pulled out of that box. One of those things was a black, two-piece string bikini. I still had pencils for legs but the top half of me had developed almost overnight. I was a tomboy until I hit sixteen when my chest said otherwise.

"That's one of the benefits of being a St.John. So, wait till it happens to you," I said, poking Wren in the side. She entertained me by sticking out her chest.

The girls' swimming class started after the boys left the pool. It may have been the last scheduled class of the day. There might have been twenty black students on campus, period. We got to know each other by default. Anyway, many of the boys stayed around the pool to watch the timid girls tread water and the braver ones somersault off the diving board into the deep end – which eventually, we all had to do.

One day, after a class, your grandfather caught up to me coming out of the locker room. He invited me to his dormitory for a party. I was as shy as a battered cat. I said I'd think about. I told my friend, Leslie, about the invitation. She had been invited too. She had a crush on him so I went for her sake.

One of the guys throwing the party handed me a cup and smiled. Your grandfather walked up and took it. He took a sip and set it down. He handed me his cup and invited me to go sit outside on the breezeway. We sat a little while before he cleared his throat.

"The guys are going to hate me for telling you this, but most of us stay after swimming class to watch you," he said.

"There are far prettier sites in that pool to see than me," I said.

"But they're not wearing that bathing suit. We bet each other whether your top will come off in the water. Not many black girls are confident enough to wear a string bikini."

Already shy, I was instantly embarrassed. I was a late bloomer into the female body, but I arrived hauling double D's. The lower half of me decided to wait, and all of me weighed under a hundred pounds. I had no idea my bathing suit was daring. It was the first I'd ever owned. What he called confidence was pure ignorance. I jumped up to go hide my little hinny in my room.

He grabbed my hand.

I snatched away and almost ran.

"Well, at least let me walk you to your dorm," he said.

I was moving so fast, he was following rather than escorting. He caught up, partly from me losing steam.

"Look," he said. "There's something else you should know." He hesitated so long I started to walk away. He grabbed my arm again. "Look, I like you. It's just that…. you are way too innocent."

"You mean way too country, don't you?"

"The cup I took from you was spiked," he said "One of us was going to hand you a drink, the other was going to do what I did, tell you some stuff girls like to hear, and wait for the drink to kick in. That person was going to take you to his room to let you lay down, and well…."

"Oh my god! Ya'll planned to take advantage of me? Who!"

"Me," he said, reluctantly.

I'm not a violent person, but I wanted to put a hole in his chest and pull his ribs out the back. Instead, fire warmed the tears that inched their way down my face and met under my chin. I rarely get thrown off my mark but that confession scrambled my brain. I must have matured five years by virtue of his admission.

About a month later, word traveled around the campus that my roommate, Blu, was the brunt of a horrible prank. Blu's face was not the most attractive but she was brilliant and had a body that would turn any man's head, and some women. As attractive as her body was, her attitude was in the total opposite direction. Truth be told, her behavior was arrogant, snobbish and nasty. We had nothing in common except the room we shared. We didn't even share hellos in our coming and going. In her mind, I was beneath her, as were most of the black students. She even told us so. Many of us were from small towns, and the first in our families to attend college. Blu was from middle class Atlanta. She studied excessively, not participating in any of the nonsensical things we did to build black solidarity on an exclusive white campus.

The rumor found its way to me. The gang that had planned to see me naked had done the same to Blu. While, in her mind, most of us were country pimples on a pig's behind, she really liked one of the boys. He knew it and played on her interest. He had invited her to his room where three other guys had hidden in the closets. As they were fooling around, one of the closet rats snickered. The guy with Blu tried to play it off but the closet rat couldn't control himself. They were busted.

As the news traveled expressway around campus, I found Blu packing. She was so angry her hair stood on her head like the spikes on a bulldog's collar. She was flinging curse words she could have taught to my Uncle Lindy. He was the most consummate curser I have ever heard; even to this day. She would have made him proud. I tried to befriend her but she turned on me like the child in the Exorcist. So I left her there, hurling poetic curse words across the room.

"That's how I met your grandfather. It didn't start well, and ended far worse. Now back on point."

Was what they did to Blu and would have done to me God's will? Why her and not me? I have never understood why they had been so cruel. One had the nerve to say, "She had it coming; the way she looks down her pickled-nose at everyone else." That would be karmic; one of the Immutable Laws. What you do to others, is already done to you in this life or the next. Some know it as 'you reap what you sow'.

Was there a memory in that experience for her? For me? For the guys? Perhaps the guy who said she had it coming was right. In her own way, she perched high like a parrot and looked down on us. Her cruelty was just as insidious, but did she deserve what they did to her? Why was I spared from a similar psychological homicide?

No one can tell me that she or I created the pain we experienced, nor that God willed it. Some will tell you *everything* is a lessons we have to learn. That's one way to process awareness. I say, there are no lessons to learn; only memories to recall about who we are, who the other is, and our relationship to each other. But God would not put it into someone's spirit to cause harm to teach anyone a lesson, or for any other reason. Still, there are things to learn and justice and mercy on every road we choose.

Ignorance allowed me to wear a string bikini, teenage hormones incited a dozen boys to line the balcony in the hopes of a wardrobe malfunction, and immaturity allowed four boys to concoct an event that left a young woman humiliated.

The inherent opportunity is to reconnect with our truth. Just think about the times you heard something and said, 'I knew that'. Some call these 'ah-ha' moments. There are times we feel something deep in our souls and know it to be right even when there is no evidence to prove it. When we come into alignment with truth, what has been forgotten vibrates in recognition of itself.

That experience allowed me to refine and strengthen my self-awareness. Perhaps the boys came face-to-face with their attitude towards women. Maybe they came to understand we are to be respected as their mothers and sisters, givers to their well-being. It could be that Blu saw her own malignant treatment of people she deemed inferior and realized that every person hurts from mistreatment the same as she did that day.

Did God *will* these events? Or did *we* orchestrate them? Many believe cruelty is a choice; a byproduct of free will like every other choice. The age-old question of destiny versus free will is all wrapped up in this story.

"Is there an answer?" Wren asked. "Seems both can be true based on everything I've heard so far, Gaia. Either God doesn't trust us if it's destiny, or we don't trust God if we apply free will. It sounds complicated."

"That's a truly insightful deduction; and it's an answer you'll have to come to on your own. Sweetheart, all I can tell you is: some say we are God's greatest creation. I believe what we do to each other is an echo of our doubt regarding that possibility."

XI

The Devil Made Me Do It

In the 1970's, comedian Flip Wilson made these words famous: "The devil made me do it!" A pint-size version of himself sat on each shoulder and gave him advice. One version wore a devil costume, the other sported a halo. Flip was conflicted, but he usually listened to the devious version because doing what that one suggested was more fun.

Most of us, at one time--or many, have blamed our missteps on some force beyond our control, or some person we feel is responsible for our predicament. We blame getting a ticket on the police officer who stopped us; when caught cheating we blame the suspicious spouse who went looking for trouble and found it; or our so-called failure on a devil that put roadblocks in our way. This Super Being has powers comparable to God, so they say.

But what if there is no devil? What if this Super Being is a figment of our parents' imaginations created to scare children into obedience? And what if, at some point, the children began to blame this demon for everything their parents considered unbecoming? And because parents can't deny the existence of this devil, this Super Being has become a lexicon in our collective culture. And as we grow, this force that is beyond our control becomes the controlling force of our lives.

"I tried that on mama once," Wren said. "She didn't buy it."

"Dang right, she didn't. What possessed you to try such a lame thing?"

"One of my classmates said that's how she gets out of trouble. She tells her mom the monster in the closet did it. Thought I'd try it."

We both laughed. "God has no nemesis, sweetness. There is no power equal, comparable, or close to the Force that is God. If there is no devil, there is no domain over which he rules. As human beings, with power over our thoughts, we co-create our experiences. Remember, we are gifted with the ability to choose one course of action over another. Sometimes, the road we've chosen leads to an outcome laden with events we could not foresee. This is because every choice has consequences and requires some degree of sacrifice. But we want to blame the devil for the so-called bad that comes with our choices. We call these events bad because we expect life to be a fairy tale where everything turns out in our favor: the guy gets the girl, the girl gets her dream and all live happily ever after. But mostly, stuff happens because we don't think it through. Life is an expanding eco-system with a cycle of duality orbiting within a constellation of events.

"Now you're speaking my language," Wren said with a smile.

"Girl, you are too smart for me. I thought for sure I'd trip you up on that one."

"Not yet, Gaia, but I like that you try," she smiled.

"Don't mess with me, girl," I said, pushing her shoulder.

Anyway, simply put, everything acts in Agreement. It goes back to the Gaia Principle. Worms tend the soil; birds eat the worms. People do good deeds; good deeds produce disaster. There is no devil waiting on the wing of the bird pointing out which worm to eat in order to punish that worm because it didn't burrow its quota of dirt.

Humans are prone to deny responsibility for their actions and decisions. Accountability is a fine line we walk as if it were a high wire act. Sometimes the balance pole tilts left, sometimes right; sometimes a small wobble, sometimes a deep dip. Should we fall, we blame the lights for being too bright, the pole for not being the right color, the rope for not being taunt enough, the audience for being too loud. It couldn't possibly be that we were not prepared, or did not approach the task with the respect and commitment it deserved. More often, we blame it on having woken up to a bad day-- as if a day has ill intent.

Deflecting responsibility is a self-protective tool and no one gets blamed for more that goes wrong in our lives as God and the Devil. God is suddenly uncaring or vengeful when a tornado decimates a town. Satan tempted us to leave our *right* mind and indulge our desires in order to claim our souls.

"That's scary stuff we tell ourselves," Wren said, seriously.

"Hold on my love." That said, there is malevolent energy. Just as the flow of love is present in the Universe, the energy of malicious intent flows too. That energy builds from the harm people do to each other. It finds its way into the stream of consciousness in our tears and on our pain. Regrets for choices made and unmade in the wake of this energy give birth to anger. Anger rises like summer heat causing a storm that forms the river of Discontent. That river spawns vengeance. Vengeance gives rise to hate. We dip and drink from that river creating more regret, forming more anger. And so it flows—the river of Discontent.

True story: Your mother's acceptance to medical school at Johns Hopkins was one of the happiest moments of my life. The sacrifices I made were offerings from my heart, all meant to arrive at that moment. I asked her father to please not bring his wife to the celebration luncheon because this was a family matter and she had shown herself to be less than friendly towards me.

Your granddad brought her anyway. She sat across the table from me at the restaurant and delivered every snide comment she must have stayed up nights rehearsing. Every one more crass than the last. She flaunted her marriage by fawning all over your grandfather. She made sure I knew what he'd done for her knowing he paid me nothing in child support. I held my p-i-e-c-e- and ignored her as long as I could.

Wren smiled.

I sat there, wondering first why he brought her and second, why he allowed her disrespect of me—the mother of his child, a child who had graduated from college with honors with little to no help from him; and was now on her way to medical school.

His collusion angered me more than her crap-filled words. But when she followed me to checkout and said something vile behind me, I dipped my hand into that river of anger and brought back a fist full of bitch-slap.

"Gaia!"

"Well, I did. Remember, I am fire. It got your grandfather's attention. He flew between us and quickly got her away from me.

The cussing I dished out bounced off everything in that lobby and made its way into the dining room. I made Uncle Lindy proud.

What followed next hurt me to my core. The pain would have been better accepted if someone had taken my liver from my un-anaesthetized body with a wooden stick. My child blamed me and proceeded to treat me so.

You can't imagine the betrayal; I hope you never do. That hurt turned into anger that demanded I remove Shannon from my eyes and ears. My exile lasted for months. I soaked in a bathtub of heavy-heart every day. Regret for all I had given up became my bedmate. It plied me with wine-laced thoughts of what might have been—if only. When I emerged, I was changed, and sadly, so was the image of who I was to your mother and she to me.

Yes, I contributed to the mayhem, but those I expected to have my back did not. I was confronted with someone drenched in malicious ill will and I was alone. Of all the things I regret about that day, putting my fist in that woman's face has not appeared on that list, ever. She chose; so did I. When met with an enemy, don't question nor justify what you're seeing and hearing. Believe them. Not everyone has good intent; they are outside their sine with God.

Wren interjected. "Mathematically speaking, the timbre of a wave is either noisy or harmonic. Sounds like she was noisy."

"Yes. And I tried to put her on a new wavelength. Sometimes you have to speak to people in the language they understand. And sometimes you have to leave them exactly where you found them."

At some point during my exile, after the pain and numbness set in, I buried my head in my pillow and just cried. I needed a place to rest my heart so it could mend. I sought the strength to accept the Truth of that experience.

The Truth: There is no devil taking over our minds and manipulating our body. There is only us, with our suspicions, regrets, judgments and anger forming the river of discontent. If you find you must take a sip from that river, drink slowly. The water there never fills you up.

XII

God is Not Meant to be Enough

"Ok, bear with me. While I am quite comfortable with my own company--and your's, my love -- there are times when I am reminded how alone I am. Today is one of those times."

"On my birthday!?" Wren pleaded.

"*Because* it's your birthday. Hear me, sweetness. I miss having someone to share special occasions like this, your birthday. I awoke this morning painfully aware that I want someone in my life who cares about what I care about. And I care so much about you that I want someone else to know and love you purely because I do."

I miss having someone who hopes for my success; who wants for me what I want for myself, someone who shares his talents, possessions, and affection to help make me the best I am meant to be. And yet, I know God created a world that supports what Abraham Maslow, a prominent psychologist in the 40's and 50's, described as a Hierarchy of Needs. The third Need is Belonging and Love, the fifth and highest is Self-actualization.

God wants us to vibrate at the level of love and happiness. That fact allows me to pick myself up and continue, to come here as happy for you as a termite in a lumber yard.

But there are times when that fact is not enough. Some days, I need someone to *say* I am good enough, and mean it, to embrace me in comfort in whatever form feels necessary. No matter how old we become, how mature we think ourselves to be, how powerful or evolved; we never outgrow the need for love, and comfort, and assurance that we are enough at that moment just as we are.

A valued friend in Cincinnati sent me an email in which he shared an upcoming vacation. Every year, a core group of guys get together and go on a fishing trip. He tells me that he and two of these men have been life-long friends. They started a mentoring program in the hopes of producing young men who will honor women, family and community as they do. Their vision is to leave a community of men, like themselves, who value something greater and will pass that on to the next generation.

The commitment to his friendships and dedication to the sanctified future of his community forced me to acknowledge that I have no constant life-long friends. I have no purposeful commitments beyond the obligations and love borne of blood.

"But you have great friends, Gaia," Wren said. "I'm really surprised to hear you say that."

Yes, I know great people I consider friends. And I believe I can call upon any one of them in a moment of physical need for some *thing*. I'm not as certain that I can call upon any one of them for emotional relief. I tried, they just looked at me funny. Perhaps I have presented myself as self-sufficient in all things to the point no one believes me. Perhaps they sense that I am different. People avoid or deny what they don't understand.

Since I was old enough to accept it, I have lived a reality that says I had to make my own way; that the people I should depend on to protect me, won't. Not my mother, not my husband, not Shannon. That knowledge imbrued my existence with strength others often misinterpret. That strength is also a weakness equal in its power to affect me.

I had a best friend in high school. Belinda and I were insepara-ble until I went off to college. She stayed home and married. We didn't see each other as much past graduation and the divergence of our lives grew with each passing event that we shared with someone else. After a while, we only heard what was happening with the other through family.

Belinda made new friends and I'm sure, became a best friend to someone else. No one filled the void she left until twenty years later when I accepted a job in Rocky Mount. On the first day of orientation, I met a woman whose presence spoke to me as if it had a voice. Meeting Carla was like meeting a twin from whom I had been separated at birth, and on that day reunited. It is no cliché to say we communicated without words. A look could pass between us that we instantly understood.

Our friendship became the source of speculation, gossip and envy. There is nothing she could have asked of me that I would not have tried to do. I'm sure she knew there was nothing she could tell me that was more protected and secure.

Our bond produced great successes for the company and the community. I was in charge of community relations. We co-hosted the most successful United Way campaign in company history to that point. That record could still stand; I don't know. I asked her to co-chair with me the first community Martin Luther King, Junior celebration. She grew it into one of the most attended city events ever. We led the company's tenth anniversary celebration, creating an experience that has never been matched. When people are in sync, or in sine, the accomplishments are profound.

When I left the plant for corporate, our friendship remained intact. By phone we laughed, we shared, we plotted. But at the nine-year mark our friendship ended abruptly. I, along with two thousand other people, was downsized from the company. I was not devastated by the news; in all honesty, I felt the change coming. We St.Johns know these things. Nonetheless, I discovered that

Carla knew this was about to happen to me and chose loyalty to the company over preparing me for the news. I truly didn't see *that* coming. I would have protected Carla's confidence as I always had. But it appeared she did not trust me in that instance. In my mind, she betrayed me. We didn't speak again for at least twelve years.

No other woman or man has been as close to me since. Is it safe to say I hardened a little? Yes, it's safe to say. But it does not mean I didn't miss her or long for who we were together. I want that kind of relationship again in my life. There is no one whose opinion I value to the degree that I valued hers during our season. Now, I keep my own counsel. My possessions enables me to see situations and people for what they are. Their truth allows me to let things go.

I have been honored to have the friendship of another soul inspired woman. Ava has been a source of comfort and support. She has gifted me beyond my capacity to return her benevolence. I love her in word and deed. But there is a distance between us that we have not bridged. It is hair thin, but is sometimes as broad as the distance between our years. Oddly, I have not tried to figure it out or to find a way to cross it. We are comfortable with each other and that seems enough.

With my guy friends, the connections don't go as deep, but are still special and I'm honored to know them. As many will attest, the relationship between people of like gender is different--like with my friend in Cincinnati and his buddies. It defies explanation. And the relationship between women is a unique thing unto itself. The memory of my life with each of them is like sunshine in November.

But today, I wept in my aloneness. Even as my Spirit friends guide me, even as I know God is never apart from me, today, God is not enough.

XIII

No Person or Situation is Ever Abandoned

"Your grandfather went to prison for bank robbery…"

Wren's eyes widened.

"Bet you didn't know that," I said, with another elbow nudge. He returned… applied for, and was accepted to medical school, becoming a distinguished physician. All along his way, those around him, those who had influence over him, saw his potential. They knew his worth before he accepted it for himself. Because others loaded him with great expectations, and because he loved a challenge, he set out to make them right.

Medical school presented ample opportunities to exercise his generous cerebral capacity and expand his curiosity. I liked that he was caring, but his big brain was really something. His intelligence, his respect for medicine and his patients made him an exceptional doctor. His charm bought him friends easily, everywhere.

But there was something in him that never accepted he was worthy of his crown. He cheated, married three times, chose not to support his biological child and created public spectacles with the alligator who had not graduated high school.

"Are you judging them, Gaia?"

"No, those are facts."

"But an alligator?"

"I call it like I see it. She reminded me of a toothless gator."

"Must be her totem," Wren said.

"See! You're paying attention!"

To seal this image of himself, your grandpa produced situations resulting in five heart surgeries leading to infections that left him disabled. Complications from diabetes, because doctors make the worse patients, caused difficulty walking. He refused to hold those causing his disabilities accountable. I believe somewhere, at a critical moment, someone told him -- no -- convinced him, he was not good enough. This allowed him to accept this maltreatment of himself and the professionals who mishandled his care. It allowed him to live as he saw himself: unable.

When I looked back on it, he was retrogressing long before I met him. It took me too long to realize I couldn't save him. Truth is, I knew that going in, but I tried anyway. The Mothers explained to me the error of my effort. That's a story for another day.

While his doubt manifested as infidelity and criminal behavior, others suffer the same doubt that shows up as drug addiction, uncontrolled gambling, sex addiction, abuse, and other social dysfunctions that leave those around them scratching their heads. How does someone with so much talent, intelligence, opportunity, or whatever, make such stupid choices? I believe they can because they don't believe they are worthy of the possessions they've been given. Others get caught up because they feel forced to do something that is not aligned with their heart's desire.

"So, how does this apply to the point that no person or situation is ever abandoned?" Wren asked.

The answer is this: God's grace is always present, yours to call upon, and to accept, at every moment, whatever the circumstance.

Even after all the high-risk medical manifestations, your grandfather did not die. He has more time to evolve. He has the gift of time to claim his worth and make amends for the disrespect of his talent and the callous treatment of your mother.

It is the same for all of us. We make decisions that lead us to divisions in the road where we are given more choices. When we ask ourselves 'what have I done? How did I end up here?' that is another opportunity to move into our potential, to expand to fit our crown. Every decision changes us, no matter what we decide. Sometimes the change supports our evolution; sometimes it appears to set us back. But, every day, every situation to make a defining choice is God saying we are not abandoned.

Unfortunately, doubt forces us to embrace *one* mistake as our worth. A musician can sell a million cds and receive awards up his tuba; but the one cd that sells fewer becomes the measure of his success. For a physician, the one patient who did not recover becomes the center of deprecation. In every case, there is a sense of not being good enough.

We've all accepted mistreatment at some point in our lives. We didn't think we could do something well so we didn't try. We took a so-called expert's advice when we knew that advice was not in our best interest. We've accepted behavior from a mate, parent, colleague, friend or child that diminished our spirit, made us believe we were not good enough and said nothing, did nothing.

Doubt is a powerful force; but it *is* man-made. It is conceived when people we trust tell us we are insufficient. It lives on the energy of that lie. Being told we are not enough can take us down a path of destruction or fuel us to greatness.

Where doubt resides is not the place we are meant to exist. My grandmother used to say: "God didn't make no junk," even as she told us how worthless we were. In her backhanded way, she taught us humility *and* self-esteem in that one sentence.

We are good enough always, and in the arms of time, we grow. The point is: we have more time, until we don't.

XIV

God Does Not Judge --
(because Truth is Temporary)

"First, let me say God's love is unconditional and never changes. Keep that in mind because this is going to be a hard one."

"Okay, Gaia. Just like you love me, right?"

"Even more. Just imagine you can do no wrong, ever, and still get everything your heart desires." Now, here goes..."

One conversation we have with ourselves is the one that compares our life to someone else's. Why is X wealthy and I'm not? Why do I struggle for everything when all C has to do is roll out of bed? We judge others unworthy of their success, or wealth, or spouse or whatever it is we think they don't deserve. The haunting question becomes: '...why not me?'

We tell ourselves that being a good person means we will be rewarded. So we define what a good person is. Typically, the person who has *can't* be a good person because we don't have. They had to have done *something* bad to get it.

I'm reminded of this guy who drank, did drugs and was not the best son or father. He barely finished high school and went from job to job, getting fired from every one. His family and friends shook their heads at his lifestyle and called him an embarrassing failure. What money he didn't drink away, he spent on the lottery—week after week.

One day, news spread that he had hit the numbers 30 million dollars worth. Needless to say, his life changed. He bought big houses that he tossed to his siblings like candy. He threw big parties, hired a butler, a driver and a publicist. Yes, a publicist. I guess he wanted to rehab his image. People questioned why *he* had won? Surely they would have been better stewards of such wealth.

Then there's the woman who could sing gibberish and affect the whole room. But she was late to rehearsal and showed up like a diva to performances. With all her talent, she was never able to move beyond local gigs while a backup singers, with a voice most considered 'just okay', secured a record deal.

Consider the businessman who cheated his partner to get the company. The husband who left his family for another woman. The woman who married for the money; the athlete who couldn't read but practiced for twelve hours a day, or the writer who spent every dollar trying to get published and got evicted from his home. We judge every one of them. But, the fact is -- they are living their truth.

Is God testing us if we do not succeed? No. Remember, the details are up to us. People who succeed do because they are not hindered by society's judgments of right and wrong. They believe they deserve it, they are consistent in their desire to have it and work to earn it. History is full of accomplishments by people who didn't play by the rules. They didn't expect success to ride in on a white horse with a ruby studded saddle and glitter in its tail.

But we judge them unworthy of their success; even some their failures because they should have quit and didn't. The lottery winner is labeled a money-wasting drug head. The businessman was going straight to hell. Conversely, we elevate to sainthood the person who played by the rules and died broken.

We don't know the heart or circumstance of the man who left his wife or what inspired the athlete. Each of us responds to life's invitations in our season. But everything there is, is available to all according to his or her talents, desire, efforts and opportunity.

"Are you saying people can do anything and it's justified because they wanted it," Wren asked.

"No, I'm saying don't judge the *doer*. Like I said before, Truth is temporary. How we perceive people and things is always changing. Most people say, 'when you know better, do better'. In essence, what we learn replaces what we know, and what we do.

There are Universal Laws. I referred to them earlier as Immutable. You can negotiate a Spiritual Law because they are of the

Spirit. They are the unspoken agreements that we make in The Sanctuary of Service. But Immutable Laws are unchangeable. One is the law of karma: 'nothing happens to you that you do not deserve whether earned in this life or the past'. In other words, you reap what you sow. That means I must have betrayed someone big time in another life because betrayal is a major theme for me now.

There are no judgments by God; rather, the consequence of our actions. Sow strife and you reap discord. Sow joy and it returns ten-fold. Treat your friends like crap and they turn on you. This is the balance of life. And if it doesn't balance in this life, maybe it will in the next, or the next. Meanwhile, there is a place where we all must atone. It's called The Temple of Tears. Immutable. There, we face and cleanse ourselves of decisions that led us out of frequency with God and away from our purpose, or caused harm to others.

"Gaia, You didn't betray anyone, ever. You're doing what God asked you to do-- you're helping them remember."

"Thank you, Wren; that's sweet of you. I hope so."

"This is a little off subject, but did you forgive grandpa?"

"Forgiveness is something we'll talk about some other time."

"I've noticed you never use his name," Wren added.

"Yes, I know, honey. It's a choice I've made. I'll come to terms with that in the Temple of Tears."

XV

God Doesn't "Do-Over"

A butterfly flapped its wings just above my head. Wren looked up at it and smiled. I cupped my ear and listened in its direction. "Okay, madam butterfly; yes, that's a good subject."

"What did it say?" Wren asked.

"She said to tell you that God doesn't do over." Hmmm... I thought for a second wondering how to share the butterfly's message. I cupped my hand to my ear again. "Okay, I got it!"

Madame Butterfly said there is no place in the whole Universe like another. That there is not a day or a minute that is the same as the one before. The same sun has never shown twice across the spectrum of time nor has the same wind touched your face. If we could measure temperature to the smallest degree measurable, we'd fine that there are no two degrees exactly the same. Even the mighty mountain changes through time.

It appears that God sees every moment as unique never to be duplicated, ever. The difference might be minor intellectually, but major in terms of the quality of the experience. God has created an elaborate system that repeats itself uniquely.

We've all probably heard that no opportunity is ever lost; that what is yours will come to you when you're ready. It's a comforting thought. But that's a fairy tale the likes of Cinderella. What the do-over mythology suggests is that there is no reason for regret; we'll get a second chance. It tells us there are no mistakes.

Well, I have regrets. There are opportunities I let go by that will not return no matter how much I wish differently. I've made mistakes, so has every person living or dead. You will too, my precious. Here is one of mine.

In my early forties, I met a Frenchman. He was some kinda cute and an unpredictable delight. Our meeting at the proverbial bar, in Indiana, was the most happenstance event ever. In that one night, we became friends and lovers. The whole event was way out of character for me, but as natural as breathing. Over the months that followed, he sent *wish you were here* postcards from wherever he was in the world. I got four page hand-written letters that endeared me to him for life.

He was an engineer and traveled across the United States troubleshooting bottling equipment. As often as possible, I met him in some of those cities. We had brunch at the Mayflower Hotel in DC, took carriage rides around Charleston, explored caves in Tennessee, made love on the Hoover Dam.

Wren grabbed her ears.

"Well, you said don't leave anything out," I laughed. We talked about everything; shared our dreams, confided our fears. Suffice to say it was the stuff of romance novels.

Fatefully, he was called back to Normandy by his company and didn't know when he would return. We had a month before he left and his last assignment was in Canada. Two week before he was to go home, he asked me to come with him to France. His offer made my heart nearly explode with happiness. And then, I panicked. I didn't speak French; what little I learned in high school was long forgotten. How would I live there? What about my job and my family? What if he changed? What if I got there and couldn't get back? Those *what ifs*, grabbed my shirttail and spun me in five different directions. A few days later, in tears, I told him I couldn't go. I never saw him again. Except in the photographs I still reminisce over from time to time.

Two years later, while tossing old papers, I came across his US contact numbers and dialed every place he had worked looking for him. There was no engineer from France. He was gone.

What I've come to understand is that every moment is an opportunity to choose. And every choice creates a unique road we follow. The chance to do, to have, to feel what was declined is gone.

Along the chosen journey might come a similar experience, but it's not the same person or the same circumstance, just a likeness of the one before. We never get to repeat *that* path we might wish we had taken. And what if France is the place I was meant to be?

Here's another example:. I purchased a vanity table and decided to change the handles. I envisioned contemporary straight lines in brushed nickel. A few weeks later, I stopped in a home goods store I had not shopped before. This was a big-box-find-everything-under-the-sun-no-hassle store. Well, you know Gaia shops with a one-track-mind. On this occasion I was looking for a runner for the bathroom.

Well, I came across the "As-Is" section of this big box-find everything-under-the-sun store, and there on a shelf were two cabinet door panels with the handles I had envisioned for my vanity -- almost; they were longer and attached differently. The best surprise is they were only ninety-nine cents each, including the door panels! I stood there pondering long enough to talk myself into walking away. I had come to buy a runner, not handles. I realized my stupidity and went back the next morning to collect my treasure only to find someone more astute had done what I had not.

Now some will say the right person got them; that those handles were not meant for me. My take away is they *were* meant for me, I had envisioned them and there they were. But I rejected them, and someone else got a bargain. Some weeks later, I found two other handles slightly different from the ones I passed by. They weren't as pretty, but no one would know they were not my first choice.

It's the same way with ideas, with love, with everything. It is there for you to discover, reveal and receive. God provided everything for each of us to prosper if we work at it. The one who responds is the one who moves closer to God's intent for us. The idea that gets acted upon is no longer available to anyone else. The love we declined is accepted by someone else. We let it pass because it didn't look exactly like we wanted, or simply weren't paying attention because our mind was focused on something else. Other partners, other ideas are out there to manifest, maybe even better ones, but not *that* one. Each idea, each experience is unique. Of course, every idea can be embellished but the concept is singularly unique. Another great love can come along, but we always remember the one we let go.

There is no word to describe how mind-blowing the notion is that God does not do over, that everything, every experience is amazingly unique -- right down to grains of sand.

XVI
All Are Gifted-- and Possessed

"Gaia, a teacher said I'm gifted. But your stories don't use the word the way I thought she meant it. I'm confused."

"Well, I'm sure she was in awe of your amazing smart self. And she probably sensed the greatness beyond your intelligence. Most people use the word incorrectly. We are gifted ... and we are possessed."

"Possessed? That doesn't sound like a good thing," Wren said.

"Trust me, it is. You, my dear, are more possessed than most," I said, smiling. "*Possessions* are qualities of the fifth element. These are things like creativity, intelligence, innate talent, sensory perceptions. Short of some unnatural catastrophe, our possessions are always with us, they're coded in our DNA. We own them; no-one can take them from us for as long as we live. When we die, we go back to Spirit, they go back to the Void. A possessions is yours to use, or not, for your benefit and the sake of others.

"A *gift* is something you have been given purely for the sake of its existence. These are not a part of you; they don't belong to you.

Beauty is a gift. Land and air exist even after we cease to be. The mountain is there whether we climb it or not. Your body is a gift. A gift is yours to enjoy--or not. Gifts are fragile. They exist in a delicate system that is contained in a mere thought."

"Can people be gifts?" Wren asked.

"Well, that's tricky." The *qualities* of a person can be a gift. But people show up with conditions and expectations we impose on each other, while a gift makes no demands. I'd rather think of people as the bearers of blessings like the wise men who brought gifts to the baby Jesus. We are not love, but bring love. Not the faith we have in each other, but the reflections of our own potential."

"Which is more important?" Wren asked.

"Well, we can exist without creating another thing; but we need air, food and people. We need to see the sky; we don't have to determine why it's blue or explore what lies beyond it.

"We don't need a computer to draw a sunset, or a telescope to see that beautiful oleander. And yet, possessions have produced our art and science and evolutions. We were designed to produce, to create; to manifest and share our possessions. In so doing, we offer our own creations as gifts to each other."

XVI1

Living on Purpose

"Let's talk a sec about the greatness your teachers see in you," I said to Wren. "You can be good doing many things. But to be great, you have to do you."

Think about this: Why would God give you life and not the resources to live? We've all heard the story of someone living on the street, an abandoned child found in a closet, or someone challenged by life in some devastating way. Later, something happens that reveals that person's brilliance in some talent or skill. Everyone says, "Amazing!"

Well, it's not amazing at all. Each of us is born with talents or skills -- our possessions -- with which we are to contribute to humanity. Some call that contribution our purpose; some call it our passion. Under the right circumstances and by sheer will, often with some degree of sacrifice, many go on to exercise that skill or talent and perform one or more of their reasons for being. Sometimes we find our mission, sometimes our mission finds us.

At very early ages children know why they were sent, and how they want to express their presence in the world. Some parents nurture that. Those children go on to become accomplished in their endeavor. You often hear them say, "I knew I wanted to do this since I was five years old," or whatever the age was. That's because they did!

Likewise, circumstances limit some children from exploring their talents or arriving at awareness of their possessions. Even so, if you ask that person what he wanted to be as a child, she can tell you. That's because somewhere in our imaginations are clues to our purpose. This group constitutes the majority of our society. They know there is something great they could have become *if only*.

In the other end of the pool are children who are forced into professions despite their discontent with doing what they are asked to do or be. You've seen or heard them. Their conversation goes something like: "I wanted to be X but my dad made me do V." Or, "It was my mother's dream for me to become Y." They have varying degrees of success but aren't happy people. Their discontent can manifest in destructive, reckless activity in one form or another. In whatever guise, their unhappiness spills out as mistreatment of themselves or the people around them.

We have guided children into professions because of the money or status or title associated with it. Some because it was the parent's failed dream. Some to follow in the parent's footsteps. We stifle our children with oughts and shoulds and nots. We distress them with the lure of something else we tell them they can be, we burden them with expectations. Finally we smother them in fear of disappointing us. Soon, they are like fish trapped in those plastic can holders.

But possessions never go away. We get reminded they are there. It's the connection we feel watching someone *doing,* or when something inexplicably captures our attention. It's that happy tickle in our belly, or a surge of regret over a dream we didn't explore. The gift is being able to recognize our talents. The challenge is to express them.

"I can't picture what you're saying, Gaia," Wren confessed.

Okay... Take your Aunt Lyn. I always imagined she'd be a fashion designer or an interior decorator. Or even a graphic artist. But for some reason she decided she wanted to be an architect. Architecture requires high level math and math is *not* her thing. She had heard the chant somewhere that she could be whatever she wanted to be. She rationalized her selection by saying designing buildings was art. I relented. She managed to do okay for a while. But after the second year of college, she faltered. She took a semester off and never went back.

No, we cannot be anything we want to be. We can try. I even accept that everything we do can be a platform to that which we are meant to be if we let it. We might even attain a measure of material success in the process. But at the heart of this topic is appreciation of who we are and what we are meant to do. It's about our value to life itself. Sadly, we've success about money and *stuff*.

Even better than Aunt Lyn, your garden is a perfect example of what I'm talking about. Different flowers are made to bloom in different regions and climates. Plant it where it's not meant to be and it might grow but will not be as fabulous as it can be, or it may not bloom at all. It might even die. But in the place it is meant to be, it becomes a thing of such beauty it moves us to the core. We actually see the face of God.

Some say if you're doing your *thing* that success comes easily; magical doors open. Well, darling, *being* takes *doing*. And doing is never without difficulties or sacrifice. Even as Moses led the people out of Egypt, they complained how hard it was even knowing God was with them. Wandering in the wilderness with that kind of noise must have been hell. But Moses was doing what he was commissioned to do. In the face of condemnation, he showed up.

Regrettably, too many people don't do because doing *is* hard; it can even be fatal. Such was the case with Malcolm X and Dr. Martin Luther King, Jr. Even Ms. Oprah has been ridiculed and sued. I've told you how life challenged Mr. Cecil. People who *do* will always be challenged by people who resent their doing. Some-one said 'life is hard and then you die'. As the Borg on *Star Trek* are famous for saying, 'Resistance is futile'. (I made a circle with one hand, placed it over one eye to simulate the Borg and spoke robot-like). Wren laughed and curled herself in hiding. "The Borg had one purpose: assimilating and transforming others in the pursuit of perfection, as they defined it."

When you *do you*, you advance God's will, and contribute to the idea of heaven. When we embrace the magnum opus of our possessions and move in the direction we are meant to go, we bloom! Or, we become nourishment for others. In some cases the doer may not experience the fruits of her labor, but has paved a path for the benefit of others. Often, their Spirit endures in cultural or political, if not tangible, ways. The names of Dr. King and Malcolm X have become synonymous with their doing. Vincent van Gogh's frequent bouts with mental illness had to be difficult but he became a famed artist who changed the art world.

When everything is in its place, when we can touch our souls and be touched, when we find joy in doing, what do we say?

This is heaven.

And so it is.

XVIII

Hell is a Room in Heaven

"What is hell, Gaia," Wren asked.

"This swing is right now; it's getting hard on Gaia's butt. Let's go back to the gazebo and those fluffy cushions."

Wren grinned and bounced off without hesitation.

Hell... A Native American proverb says 'Religion is for people who believe in hell; spirituality is for those who've been there'. The Mothers call that proverbial place, *The Temple of Tears*.

Jesus is said to have spoken, "In my Father's house are many mansions." Sooo, what if Hell is one of those mansions? What if it is a place created as another opportunity for us to understand our place in humanity? To know pain and suffering? A place to grow into our higher self? To cleanse our souls.

Hell is always painted as a place of torment. Worms breed in our organs, and demons eat our flesh. Fire blisters our skin and pain is never-ending. This is the punishment for what many call sin. But I find it difficult to believe that God would discard anything God created. If the naked mole rat and the wolf spider didn't get the boot, nothing will. Have you seen those things! They are the gift you look at and say 'What the bleep am I suppose to do with this?"

Wren giggled. "I got one of those today," she said.

"I know, I saw it. Lucky you." I laughed.

Anyway, the place where we all atone is The Temple of Tears. Some find themselves there while living; all will journey there when we transition. It is a part of our transcendence.

Every religion I know has a salvation ideology. They speak of it as being saved from the pains of life or from the punishment of sin. Redeem means to reclaim. Religion tells us there is redemption from hell. If that is true, why wouldn't God provide a redemptive space just as God provides for every other element of our existence?

Wren stopped me. "But what about punishing people for bad things?"

"Remember, cruelty is man-made. We have constructed social and civil laws meant to help us learn to support and protect each other's right to be and do and live. For the most part, they work, using the principles of reward and punishment."

But people want to impose upon God their own constructs and behaviors. Because we punish, we tell ourselves that God also punishes us for sins. If a person ends up blind or crippled, or bankrupt there must have been a big sin somewhere. Not so. Sweetheart, the idea of creation is perfect; the execution can get a little wonkie sometimes, like one of your experiments.

But here's the thing: Sin means something entirely different. *All* of creation has a unique vibration that connects us to God. Scientists refer to this as a frequency or signal. The Mothers told me that sin is *an interruption in the signal*; we have moved out of our unique frequency with God. Out of frequency, we forget who we are. When we've moved away from the Source, we're out of sine -- that is sin. It lessens our capacity to see others as ourselves; they become objects to be used. For some, the interruption is chemical or psychological -- some kind of defect they may or may not have chosen. Here is where we invoke the words Jesus spoke when He was crucified: "Forgive them, for they know not what they do."

We are free to live out of frequency, as most of us often do. It doesn't mean that God has some horrible punishment waiting for us. However, neither does it mean that we won't encounter karma. No one passes through life without paying for some poorly conceived decision, without some measure of recompense.

When people condemn each other to hell, they are partially correct in doing so. The Mothers helped me to understand that hell—The Temple of Tears— is the space in which we face our greatest regrets, see the harm we caused and the misfortune *we* created. So it is perfectly right to request someone go there. But thankfully, somewhere between hell and eternity, we heal.

XIX

God does not Require Service to God, but Sacrifice for Others

"How do we serve God?" Wren asked.

There is nothing... nothing that God has need of from us. God created everything Seen and Unseen, Known and Unknown, in every dimension, on every plane into eternity, from a mere thought. Even the first word God uttered is said to have produced life. I believe God already created everything we will ever know and discover throughout human existence within an evolutionary system. That begs the question: what can *we* do to elevate God?

"I know, I know," Wren said, and yells out: "Nothing!"

Exactly! And yet, we create all kinds of rituals and rules, sing songs and erect buildings as tokens to God. Some even label these things divine and place them above the needs of people. They worship their own creations. That said, expressing gratitude is something quite different.

Some will argue that the Ten Commandments say that God demands worship because the first commandment says, "I am God". The second commandment says: "You shall have no other gods" (small "g", plural). The third says, "You shall not take the name of God in vain". Well, let's examine these three.

My friend, Ava, has an only grandchild, whom she loves from the depth of her soul. The grandson is smart and handsome and has the world available to him because his mother and grandmother made it so.

On one eventful visit, the grandson informs Ava that his girl-friend is pregnant. The girlfriend has a husband from whom she is separated and a five-year-old child. Ava is furious. To make matters worse the girlfriend can't afford a divorce. This means her grandson's child will legally belong to the girlfriend's husband.

"Sounds like Twister," Wren said.

Yep... Needless to say, Ava is distraught over the whole situation. But shortly before the baby is due, she swallows her pain and pays for the divorce; there is a wedding, and the baby is born. Ava takes one look at him and her heart now belongs to this little thing who can barely open his eyes. He is beautiful, and smart, and loved by his father. And Ava loves her grandson all over again for the man this baby has produced.

According to the Bible, there are only three things God asks of us. The Book of Micah says these things are: 'To act justly, love mercy, and walk humbly with God'. The prophets of most religions have said it differently, but they all amount to the same. The first two obligations tell us to serve others. The third is meant to improve our own state of being. They cover the whole ten commandments. These are the Holy Trinity

"Explain, please, Gaia."

To Act Justly. The Golden Rule is a dogma of the Christian faith. "Do unto others as you would have them do unto you." It sounds noble on the surface. Unfortunately it has caused much discord among civilizations because everyone sets themselves or their group as the standard for what is acceptable behavior. According to the Mothers, what the Golden Rule really says is, 'Do unto others as "I" have done unto you'. The "I" meaning God. This is just. Ava accepted her grandson's choices and acted in his favor.

Mercy is sister to justice. Acts of kindness and compassion allow us to empathize and they prepare the heart to forgive. Mercy allows us to bless another. Ava showed compassion for the baby's mother. Her heart showed kindness even as her head judged the situation untenable.

To Walk Humbly means to be in sine with God, to do so without arrogance or pride, to recognize there is something beyond our understanding, and to respect that which animates all things.

Not one commandment demands worship of God, but a recognition that there is *only* God. God is saying to us, 'I am God. There is no other but I, there is nothing but I. There is no thing that is not

I. I am all that is'. I am the Seen and Unseen, the Known and Unknown. Because this is true, God has no need of anything from us. It would be like giving a drink of water to the ocean.

The other seven Commandments tell us to feel an adoring regard for each other. Adoration allows us to sacrifice. It produces selfless good deeds for the well being of others. We can surrender short term loss for a greater gain. Think of a parent who chooses a child's needs over the lure of a promotion with greater demands, or the boost to esteem from a shiny new car. Imagine a person who has saved for years for a trip to Europe but gives the money to a stranger whose house burned down days before. Some even accept death as their gift for the advancement of others.

Ava surrendered to the situation. Rather than resist, and scream and berate, she surrendered to adoration for her grandson. She sacrificed to pay for a divorce. She made it possible for her grandson to have full claim to his child and for the baby's mother to be free of her past. Now, this beautiful new baby has a mother and father together. He has a life filled with honor and love.

Even as God commands we honor each other, we are told not to worship people, or images. We are not to revere *things*. Mind you, there is nothing wrong with things. They add to our lives and help us wear our crown. Oftentimes, the *things* we worship are ideas or expectations in our own heads. Ava put the future of her great grandson above the *image* of what her grandson's life should be. She expanded the possibilities for this new father and her family.

The third commandment tells us 'do not take the name of God in vain'. 'In vain' is odd phrasing, but consider this: We are the thoughts of God, created to interact with other thoughts of God in Truth and Love, because this is what God is. So, to deceive is to dishonor God. To disrespect another, is to disrespect God. To wrongly use God's name -- for example, to damn or harm another in God's name -- is unthinkable. In order to damn, there must be judgment. God is Truth and Love, Beauty, Adoration, Kindness, Mercy, Justice and so on. To see ourselves otherwise shows contempt for the presence of God in each of us and all of Creation.

God is God and has no personal or emotional needs. Instead, God has asked us to nurture our own character and care for one another. Eight of the ten commandments bear this out.

Ava spoke her feelings truthfully. She humbled herself; she acted justly and mercifully; she honored God. As a result, a new truth evolved.

This brings me back to the beginning: God needs nothing of us for God's sake, but requires us to surrender to each other for their elevation and our own.

XX

God Does Not Belong to You

I often hear people exclaim *their* God did something miraculous for them: healed sickness, took the taste of alcohol from their mouths, gave them the perfect job; stopped a speeding bullet.

I'm not debating the truthfulness of what they claim, only that they *own* the God that did it. When people take ownership of God, the next step is to try and give that God to someone else so that their God can do the same for the new customer. It makes the giver feel special. 'Do you need forgiveness, help with your addiction, to find the love of your life, to get out of that abusive relationship, a new job? Here—use my god! What he did for me, he'll do for you'.

God is put in a bottle and peddled like a miracle drug. They have made God a commodity whose price is ten percent plus tax.

Those in the last minutes of hope about to board the bus to despair hear this peddling and pay their tithes as the price to get God's attention. Then comes the fine print: they have to keep praying and paying. If God in the bottle doesn't give them the desires of their heart, they're not praying correctly. If they didn't get that big house or luxury car, either they withheld something from God, or it's not their time to have it. It's on the way; it got held up in shipping. 'Just wait on the Lord'. Many religious groups claim to have the only *true* God. Their religion is the Swiss Army knife of life. They are the *true* believers and only through *their* faith can you reach heaven. These groups might afford you the courtesy of calling you, superficially, a child of God. But unless you believe as they do, your soul is damned for eternity. Perdition awaits.

The desire for happiness, whatever defines it, is hardwired in our spirit because God instilled it there. The kingdom of God is *Joy*.

All of us need love and recognition. That appears to be hard-wired, too. Many people turn to religion as the source for satisfying these needs. The peddler has promised them the love of God and a family of supporters who call themselves the body of Christ. All you have to do is follow the rules.

Don't get me wrong. I am not indicting the peddler or the patron. The patron needs help, no doubt, and wants to live the promise of heaven. And the best peddler is the one who has had a first-hand God-inspired experience. The need to share good news is equally hardwired as a side effect of the experience.

The point I'm trying to make is that God cannot be owned and is not the exclusive property of any person or faith. There is no denomination absolutely right or wholly wrong in its practice.

Despite how that worship might appear to an outsider, all paths lead to God. The only difference is the traveler and the journey.

I've got another story. There was a Holiness church in the neighborhood where I grew up. The women members wore long dresses and covered their hair with scarves. They never wore makeup, not even nail polish. They believe true beauty comes from within. One of their rules said no dancing to secular music.

"Sounds a bit stiff," Wren said.

"Not after they got filled with the holy ghost," I said. They shouted up one isle and down another. Skirts just'a flapping. One or two would trip so they just jerked on the floor in the spirit.

Lyn's best friend was a member of that church. She would come by our house and they would play with makeup – lipstick and dust powder mostly because those were the only beauty products Mama had.

"What's dust powder?" Wren asked.

"Well, back them, that's what we called face powder. I don't think we had foundation. Just that dry beige dust they patted on their faces. It was a while before it came in shades of brown. Some even used the talcum powder they put on their babies' butts."

"Oh." is all Wren could muster.

"Yep. Seeing those faces is probably why your Gaia doesn't wear makeup today," I said.

Anyway, When they became older, late teens, Lyn's friend began wearing mini skirts and going to nightclubs.

The church pronounced her demon-possessed. Owning God gives the owner the right to judge, the right to insert themselves in other people's lives, the right to condemn. Lyn's friend was forced to undergo a laying on of hands. They were going to put God back into her through prayer and speaking in tongue to lock God in.

Well, it didn't take. She still liked wearing makeup and dancing. When all their prayers didn't turn her back into one of them, she was shunned. Eventually, she stopped going to church.

No one can give God to you. There is no ritual that will get you a special audience to make God's acquaintance. Likewise, no one can take God from you. God cannot be repossessed if you fail to pay the weekly price of admission. God is every blink, every heartbeat, every smile, every tear; every ounce of love you give or get. Trust that you are a thought of God and that every experience—whether it's smelling a flower, or talking to a burning bush—is holy.

Even dancing.

XXI

It's Not What You Take In; It's What You Send Out

I have several friends who will not read, listen to or watch anything that does not have God's name in it. They eat only according to some rule and perform according to some ritual; certain activities are strictly forbidden. They exist in a box built of restrictions. They fail to recognize that the soul is as safe in the body as it is in the heaven they seek.

On one hand, I get it. Discipline is as important to faith as it is to life. Discipline allows us to focus. Discipline breeds consistency and comfort. Consistency is the hallmark of proficiency. Doing our best leads us towards perfection.

On the other hand, I wonder how fragile their faith must be. I'm the first to admit that cursing adds no value to a conversation, generally. But sometimes, a choice curse word best makes the point. In that instance, the word carries truth.

But in my opinion, those who withhold anything from themselves or others purely for the sake of ritual are missing the point. Denial for the sake of denial doesn't put them closer to God. Acceptance of others' truth without judgment, and the courage to share our own, just might.

XXII

We are the Sum of Our Imperfections

I have skinny legs. Growing up, they were the source of my bane, producing such nicknames as bird and chopsticks. My grandmother, unlike me, had the most beautiful legs I have ever seen. They were full and shapely, without a hint of flaw. Not a scratch or a bruise, and she worked every field that grew a crop of anything. Up to the day she died, when the rest of her had relinquished to time, her legs refused to follow. I wanted those legs.

Along with toothpick legs my heart was as soft as baby chicks. Sentimental movies meant to tug at the heartstring yanked until I gushed. I cried if a bird flew into a car or a worm dried up on the sidewalk. I even cried if the Road Runner dropped a cliff on the Coyote. For that, I was called too sensitive.

When I was older, a friend asked what I would change about myself. I pretended to think about it and finally said, "My legs." He narrowed his eyebrows to say, "What?"

"They're skinny," I said, and spilled my childhood taunts. When I was done, he got a Polaroid camera, the predecessor of cell phones today, and snapped my legs. He fanned the square card that had wheezed from the camera, looked at it a few seconds and handed it to me.

"There is nothing wrong with those legs that I can see," he said.

"For the first time, I actually *saw* my legs. They weren't as full and flawless as grandmothers', but they had the same contour, only smaller in circumference and darker in tone. Their size made sense since I barely weighed 100 pounds.

I was reading and came across the word wabi-sabi. It's a Japanese word that means finding beauty in imperfections and profundity in nature. It celebrates the blemishes and crevices that mark the evidence of what time leaves behind. It reveres simplicity and authenticity and acceptance of what is and what isn't.

I still cry over images of abused animals, saccharine movies and sentimentalities. I get that words matter and actions have long lasting effects. I have never called anyone a malicious name nor taunted a flaw in their physiology or mentality that would hurt their esteem.

I learned to see myself in truth rather than insecurity. I do not compare myself to others. I accept what might be label imperfections, are a design unique to me and perfect to God.

Wa Sabi.

XXIII

God Has Given Us Each Other to Show Us Who We Are

"Wren, Gaia needs a break. How about this: I'm going to sit out the next litany. It's about family. And the perfect story is in my computer. Let's go to the lab; you can read it for yourself."

"Okay, that sounds good, Gaia," she said.

Inside, I clicked on the folder and opened the file. "A client invited me to speak at her family gathering. Emma was struggling with her role after their mother died. Her mother's spirit provided me guidance that helped her daughter better understand her place in the family.

"Emma had recently completed a master's degree and invited her siblings and friends to celebrate the milestone with her." I moved from the seat and let Wren take my place. "I'll be back shortly." This is what she read:

Family. Everyone has one. A mother and father. Aunts and uncles. Sisters and brothers, usually. We all have some idea of what it means to be a member in a family. That meaning is often as different as the number of people you're related to. So, what is Family?

When Emma asked me to speak at this gathering, I had no idea why I was chosen. I've never thought myself to be that versed on the subject, nor have I been the traditional family member. I wanted to understand as much as I could about your mother and the family dynamics. So I looked to your mother for inspiration. I talked with each sibling and Emma let me look through her family albums to get a sense of you and your mother's presence.

What your mother and those photos inspired me to tell you is this: A family is a living organism made up of unique individuals whose purpose is to support, protect, nurture and elevate each other. This organism replenishes itself; it sheds, it grows and expands. It is bound together by blood, but held together with love.

Whether we are family by blood or friendship, some of us make it our business to hurt the person who shares our name. We withhold something, or we criticize and point fingers when one of us is suffering or fails to meet expectations.

We forget that we all go though our Valley Of ____. It might be the valley of regret, loss, betrayal, drugs, hurt, illness; even the valley of death. But that is exactly when families need each other for Support. Rather than judge it, or criticize how the person got in that situation, as a family member, our duty is to let our sister or brother, cousin, uncle, or niece know there is recovery on the other side. We stand in for them until they can stand for themselves. .Support and protect, nurture and elevate.

I believe that even before you were born God gave you the gift of this family and people who care about you. God gave you qualities and skills; ways, and means to allow you to express who you are. Then God whispered into your ear these two words: Do You.

That is both an invitation and a challenge. To be the best member of the family you can be – *Do You.*

A friend of mine works as a property manager. She shared a story I'd like to share with you. A couple of weeks ago, a tenant who was about to be evicted came in with her boyfriend. For privacy reasons, because he was not on the lease, the boyfriend could not be involved in the conversation with the tenant. At this point, she turned to him and said, "Don't worry, I got this." My friend tells me he said back, "Do you, Baby, do you." The friend had no prior knowledge of this tenant; she had just taken over management and was simply concluding the eviction process. She braced for a tirade. Turned out the tenant was a smart, reasonable person who had had some temporary difficulties.

So, how do you – *Do You*? More than anything else, know who you are. That tenant effectively presented herself in that conversation. Because she showed up as who she is, with her truth, everything turned out fine, so fine she didn't get evicted.

How do you nurture and support, protect and elevate? *Do You.* We all come into our families with the perfect possessions that are exactly what we need to share with each other and earn our living in the world. But when we let others tell us that we are a "B" or a "D" or a this or a that, those words can cloud our greatness. When you try to live your life *like* somebody else, or *for* someone else, you weaken your power.

In order to do you, trust yourself. When you trust that God made you for a reason, nobody can fillet your spirit like deboning a fish. They might nick you trying; but when you know your greatness, you do great things. Even the smallest deed has value.

When you *Do You*, when you give the world who you are, the Universe responds likewise, expanding your presence. If you don't know who you are, try this: When you are alone with yourself, thinking your thoughts, the person that shows up in that space is the authentic you. It is up to each of us to give one another the space to be who we are. Our duty is to Protect those God has entrusted in our care as they grow into their crown.

To *Do You*, you must have confidence and self-worth. Confidence is not arrogance, but humility; self worth does not bully, but lifts up.

To Do You, you must know the power of your words. I had dinner with another friend recently and I was going on about a woman who had gotten me riled up. It had taken me a while to get there, but I was sufficiently pissed. My friend interrupted and said, "Are you familiar with a study a scientist named Dr. Masaru Emoto did on water?" Needless to say, I cocked my head to the side with that *excuse me?* look on my face while my friend told me this story. He said:

Dr. Emoto took glasses of ordinary water from the same source with the same amount of water in each glass. He looked at the water under a very powerful microscope. All of the glasses showed the components that make water, water. What the cells of water were made to do, they did. He photographed these as his base study.

The experiment began. I suspect the story has changed over time but the results have not. In my friend's version, Dr. Emoto bought in a monk who chanted in front of one glass of water. After the allotted time, Dr. Emoto looked at the water under this powerful microscope. He was amazed. The cells in the water were moving differently.

For the second experiment, an ordinary person spoke the words: "thank you" to the next glass. The results were more amazing. Dr. Emoto saw these beautiful crystal-like formations; like snowflakes.

In the third test, a different person spoke: "I love you" to the third glass of water. Under the microscope, not only did the cells reshape into these new formations, they glowed.

Dr. Emoto didn't bring in another person because he postulated that the water could be changing because of the unique voice vibrations of the person speaking to the water. That the water was responding to sound waves.

So, this time, he brought in another scientist to observe. Dr. Emoto wrote on a piece of paper and sat it beside the last glass of water. He asked his colleague to examine the water under the microscope. She was speechless. The electrons in that glass of water were agitated; they moved about frantically. She asked Dr. Emoto what was written on the paper. He went into the room and got the piece of paper and showed it to his colleagues. The words on that paper said: "You make me sick."

What makes Dr. Emoto's study so powerful is this: Humans are 70 percent water! Don't you just love his name. Words affect us just as they did the water in those glasses.

There is a proverb that says sticks and stones may break my bones but words will never hurt me. It's not true. My friend was reminding me that words have power. Mothers, be mindful of the words you use on your children. God spoke something special to them. I guarantee you those words were not you're stupid, you make me sick, or shut up. Words and events can shape a child, becoming the filter through which they see themselves and others.

Men, the words *thank you*, and *I love you* had a profound effect on the water. Think about the change it can have in your wives or girlfriends and children.

Our duty is to Nurture each other with love. And sometimes, love means saying no. As parents, we can give children so much that we send them out into the world with no core. We've all seen them, know them. They don't think they should work for what they get and expect life to be easy. The first challenge and they fall apart. It is by our character that others know who we are. "No" can be excellent soil in which to nurture those virtues.

When you Do You, when you know who you are and trust the Truth of who you are, when you are confident in that Truth, you do

God's will for your life. Often we don't share the truth of who we are because we don't trust each other to protect our truth. We fear their judgment and condemnation.

So what does it look like when you know who you are? Take this family for example. There were twelve sisters and brothers. Each as different as stars in the sky. But each brings a unique quality to the family dynamic.

1. Sister A – when her children were small, they were never out of arms' reach. They are adults now and she still keeps a watchful eye. She has and continues to protect them. I'm told she can take a dime and make a dollar; a dollar and make a hundred. In both ways, she is a protector.

2. Brother B – is a philosopher. He has gone beyond the boundaries of physical earth (I won't say how he got there), but he explored the nature of God and man. This brother is a wise man. Because he has seen what most do not understand, he shows us the *joy* of living. Watch him dance and you know what I mean.

3. Brother C – This brother was the first to leave the family circle. But I learned that there was never a stranger in his presence. He gave freely and from his heart to everyone. He

was an example of openness and compassion.

4. Sister D – represents bravery. She is ready and willing to fight for what she believes. I know if any of the family ever needs her, she has your back. She'd step in harm's way to defend you and those she consider a friend. She is a warrior.

5. Brother E – Many of you may not know this, but E is one of the smartest people in this room. He is skilled in math and seems to pull answers to problems right out of the air. But smart men in our society have a very hard time because intelligence in black men is not respected.

6. Your sister, Emma – whom we celebrate — nurtures this family. She cares for each of you separately and collectively. She is the family's heart. She brings the spirit of giving in her cooking, the sacrifices she makes, and the support she provides without question. Ask her to come, and she's there. Ask her to do and it's done.

7. Sister G –provides opportunities to question what is right and wrong. Many times, we tend to shade life in gray for everything. Well, there are times when there are only two choices: yes or no, right or wrong, do or don't. And once

she's chosen, there is no turning her around. A family needs decisiveness.

8. Brother H – has amazing promise as an artist. An artist is one who sees the beauty, or ugliness, in the world and can reflect that back in a way that gives us pause. Rather than pencil and paper, he now shows his art through music. His talent allows us to feel who we are inside.

9. Brother I – demonstrates responsibility. I have never met a man more committed to his family than this brother. It can be easy to do the right thing when times are good, but in rough water he does not waiver. He works diligently to provide for those under his care. He provides not only to his family, but to his employees looking to do the same.

10. Brother J – is the seeker. He will ask a dozen questions looking for answers. He shows us that we should never accept what is obvious, or what someone tells us is truth; rather, find that truth for ourselves. But the quality I'd like to point out is his humor. He can make you laugh— even at yourself. A family needs laughter.

11. Sister K – wears the gift of grace. She is slow to speak but is passionate when she does. She represents tolerance and

patience. I am in awe of her grace as she's gone through her Valley of ….

12. Lastly, Brother L -- represents reflection. He is able to look at himself from the outside in. He sees where he needs to grow and begins a journey in that direction.

This family is Protective, Wise, Compassionate, Brave, Smart; Nurturing, Discerning, Talented; Responsible; Humorous, Graceful, Reflective. Say this family's name and it means something. It has an identity, a reputation that is known and respected throughout the community.

To this family, to *any* member of *any* family, I say: live God's command to Do You. How do you do that?

1. Be true. Know and accept who you are.

2. Trust that God made you to fulfill a role in your family.

3. Share your possessions.

4. Believe that you are enough.

A family is a living organism of unique individuals whose purpose is to support, protect, nurture and elevate each other. To be the best member of the family you can be –do you—and accept with assurance that who you are is enough.

XXIV

Time Is Not a Salve

History doesn't change – only our willingness

to tell the truth about our past.   *- mebsmith*

Wren had closed the file and was watering an amaryllis when I returned. If all went well, it would bloom in December. After getting something to fortify me, I was ready to tell the next story.

"I liked that story," she said.

Well, on the subject of family, I'd like to tell you about two women I know. Shirley and Kindra were very different people in character and personality. I am different from them and yet we shared an all too common path.

I didn't know Shirley personally. We worked on the same floor of the company. She was in Finance and I in Human Resources. She was quiet, soft-spoken and always pleasant. She was deeply religious, almost pious but didn't wear her faith like a cleric's collar, more like a gentle perfume.

Kindra was my niece by marriage. Your grandfather and her father are brothers. Her mother and I were pregnant for some of the same months. Kindra came first by a few weeks. I remember thinking what a beautiful child. She looked like soft dark chocolate.

She had dimples so deep, they almost met each other when she smiled. A shiny flock of hair curled around her face and made her glow. Everyone said she looked like something from heaven, and she did. In fact, her parents nicknamed her Angel.

Kindra grew in leaps, literally like a weed and stayed that way; tall and lanky all her life. She was funny, and rambunctious, and just a delightful child. When Shannon was around nine, I divorced her dad and we moved away. I only saw Angel on rare occasions after that. I don't know what kind of woman she grew to be.

Shirley left work that Friday and went home to an unthinkable fate. Her husband beat her to death with a baseball bat. He destroyed her face, shattered her legs, and dislocated a shoulder. All her ribs were broken. She had massive internal bleeding. Some of her brain was spooned from the walls into a Ziploc bag. She was thirty-one years old, mother of two.

In a fight with her boyfriend one Wednesday morning, Kindra was stabbed repeatedly. The father of her child had been arrested before for violence against her. He vowed if he went to jail again it would be for a *real reason*. She ran to her father's bedroom where she collapsed, and drowned to death on the blood in her punctured lungs. Her one-year-old son was found in the bed where his mother died.

They lived short lives

And lived them hard.

A life of pain

To die in vain

By the men they chose to love.

What happened to them happens every day, somewhere to someone. When someone kills another like this, the abuser is called an animal. How unkind to whatever animal they are likened to. Animals, in the natural order of things, kill to eat. When left no alternative they kill to protect. Now that we're civilized, men call their violence football, hunting, boxing, wrestling; even business. At its highest, they call it war.

When raw and untamed, it is Shirley's broken body and Angel drowning on her blood.

The truth is, any person, under the right circumstance can do unspeakable, or courageous things they might not do otherwise.

My heart has hurt for Angel -- not entirely because she was family, but because I've placed on her the pain of violence visited upon women and children in the name of love. I hurt for her because I know the pain she endured. I am reminded that it could have been me.

I remember the arguments between your grandma, Nola, and the man she married. Many of these sessions ended with broken furniture and torn clothes. Our furnishings were twice removed from being called modest to begin with. Still, most everything, over time, ended up repaired, patched, glued or covered. That is what we do; we cover up the evidence of our inhumanity like that. We stick it back together with glue.

One of the most vivid memories I have growing up is when my stepfather put a shotgun in my mother's face and said he'd blow her head off her shoulders. She dared him to pull the trigger. Dillon and I were there. I was fourteen years old; Dillon may have been ten. I stood there wondering why she would dare him to kill her.

Dillon and I jumped between them trying to take the gun from our stepfather. He drew the gun on Dillon. I stepped to him and said, "If you hurt my brother I'll kill you." I said it with such certitude that it surprised him. Shoot, it surprised me. That kind of defiance was not in my nature at the time. I was the shy, quiet one. He stood still for a minute, looking at me, then put down the gun. "Don't you ever hit my mama again," came out next. It was an order just as the other was a statement of fact. He stared at me, got his keys, into his car, and drove off. They still argued after that, but I don't recall him ever hitting her again.

I desperately wanted to leave home, to be away from the abuse, from the yelling and whippings I got from Nola. As the oldest, the younger ones were my responsibility. Your aunt Lyn broke a brand new lamp. I got the whipping. Dillon wet the bed, I cleaned him up and changed the sheets.

The mother-daughter talk I got was: "If you ever let a boy up your dress I'll put your head on a chopping block." She threatened to kill me. Imagine that. Those words went deep.

A chopping block, in this case, was the trunk left when a tree was cut down. It was used to hold logs for splitting into smaller pieces with an ax or a hatchet. This was the summer before my seventeenth birthday. The classmate who walked me to the store for ice cream asked to take me to a movie. I had never been out on a date at the time. I had heard girls at school talk about the fun they had had on any given weekend. It never crossed my mind that his invitation was that. None of it interested me.

Of course, there were the fights between boys over some girl thought to be his territory. These usually amounted to little more than threats and pushing. The fights between girls for the same offense were often exceedingly worse.

I had seen what men do to their wives, what boyfriends did to their girls and what girls did to each other. No, I had no interest in dating. I was content reading about far away places and unusual people in as many books as I could check from the library.

I often hid out in a grove of trees at my grandmother's house or in the cemetery across the road. It was quiet, serene. There was peace. At seventeen, this was my world and yet, my mother found it necessary to say those words to me.

Nola had me at seventeen. In adulthood, I realized she was protecting my promise of college out of fear that I would do the same. She drew upon violence because that is what she knew.

Two years later, I married your grandpa. I should have listened to the ancestors who tried to warn me; but I didn't. After the third attempt, we made it to the Justice of the Peace. The very day after, my new husband slept with another woman. It was the beginning of ten years of emotional abuse and the introduction of several women into my marriage. When the words had no more effect, he became physical. Through it all, I heard Mr. Cecil's words, 'Don't let nobody turn you around'.

"Why did you marry him, Gaia," Wren asked.

Well, I was nineteen and had rarely dated; what did I know, except he was brilliant, and funny, and handsome. I loved the way he danced. On the floor, we fit. And in a card game of whist, we were a force to reckon with. I cared about him. At his core was compassion and loyalty for his friends. He shared his soul with me. Despite our past, I still hold his confidence in trust.

I vividly recall the last time I was hit by the man who fathered your mother and claimed to love me.

Wren interrupted. "He loved you, Gaia, he just didn't know how to show it." I smiled weakly, knowing she was right. And no one knew the dangers of ignorance better than me.

We separated. He was home from medical school visiting his mother and drove up to see Shannon. To give them time alone, I had accepted a dinner invitation with a co-worker —who was gay, by the way. His partner was out of town and he could see I needed a friend.

When I got home, the questions began. They were harmless at first, like: "Did you have a good time". In short order, they grew into anger that morphed into violence. He punched me in the head. I fell onto the sofa. He yelled something and grabbed my arm. I collected myself enough to tell your mom to go to the neighbor's apartment across the hall. Shannon stood wide-eyed watching her father jerked me up from the sofa by my collar. She had never seen him like this; I had to scream at your mom to leave.

As she ran, he dragged me to the kitchen, took a knife from the block and said, "Scream again and I'll cut your heart out." We made so much noise I was sure the neighbors would call the police. Meanwhile, I fought with all I had. I managed to get to the bedroom and locked the door; the telephone was there. His fist tore through the door like the cardboard it turned out to be. He yanked the phone from the wall and punched me in the back with the handset. The pain tore through me like an electric shock. I fell onto the bed hard. My eyes were cloudy, my mouth was bleeding and my ears rang. He straddled me, pinning me to the bed. Through clenched teeth, he said: "Look at me; I'm the last thing you'll ever see." He put his fingers around my throat. I struggled against the pressure, clawing at his hands. I couldn't speak or scream; tears streamed down the sides of my face. Everything went black.

The space around me became a tunnel. At one end was the scene of my husband pressing his full weight upon my throat. On the other was a radiant, peaceful light. It was bright as the sun but didn't hurt to look at it. Curiosity led me in its direction, but I wasn't moving physically.

Before I reached the light, a Voice spoke to me. It was neither male nor female. We conversed and somewhere in the conversation, I asked, "What will become of my daughter?"

The Voice said, "Whatever you support her becoming. Go back. Your time is there."

"I can't go back," I said to the Voice, "Look," pointing at my body, lifeless on the bed.

The Voice said again, "Go. All will be as it should."

Back in my body, my husband's hands were still around my throat but I no longer felt them. I spoke in a voice as calm as pass the butter. "Take your hands off me, " I said.

He stared at me, confused and surprised. He loosened his grip. I repeated the words. He got up. I could see the realization of what he had just done on his face. I sat up. I had no strength to make him leave, but I found power. He tried to speak but the only word he managed was "I..." He turned and walked out of the room. I heard the front door close and he was gone. Two years passed before I saw him again.

No one had called the police. I got your mom and put her to bed. Amazingly, I slept well that night and went to work the next day. I was sore all over but I felt fine. My manager came to my desk shortly after I arrived. I saw the expression of my truth on his face. Sympathy filled his voice. He sent me home and told me not to return until the doctor said it was okay.

In the car, I looked in the mirror. Every blood vessel in my eyes must have ruptured. The flesh underneath was green, purple and blue. I had not seen any of that before. I cried for the first time--a deep guttural, pain-filled cry. After leaving the doctor's office, I saw my optometrist, and called an attorney. The divorce decree came a year later two days before my birthday.

The neighbor who took Shannon that night and kept her after school refused to keep her anymore. It was just Shannon and me. I would leave work to meet the bus, make sure she was inside and then go back to work. I'd call every thirty minutes for the two hours she was home alone.

Later that summer, I was transferred to second shift. The company knew of my situation and I think they did it to force me to leave, or because they simply didn't care. Family friendly policies were just friendly words at the time and women, especially black woman, were not wanted in industry, certainly not as managers by the white men we supervised.

I made one of the hardest decisions of my life. In order to keep that job, I had to separate my baby from me. I took her to live with Nola. Thoughts of momma leaving Dillon, Lyn and me to live with Grandma Alice for the same reason visited me in my waking days and haunted my sleeping nights. I knew momma was not grandma, but I still wondered if she resented taking care of Shannon. I certainly resented her having to. I chose the husband who created this situation and my human self surely resented him.

I could have been Kindra or Shirley. For a brief moment I was. In looking back, Kindra's environment did not support her resistance. She was born and raised into a family that pushed and hit. There were five brothers and every one of them beat their wives. There were three sisters to these brothers and their husbands hit them. I later learned that their father beat their mother, but she ultimately became the aggressor. I vowed to the God in Shannon that I would not allow her to see another moment of abuse in our home, especially abuse of me.

I have thought for many years about what separates me from Shirley and Kindra, and what made me one of them. I know each of us has a greatness that scared those men. Thy wanted it gone. Why? Because they didn't feel worthy of our gifts to them. Perhaps we wanted someone to love us in a way we didn't feel loved as a child. The person who said the words convincingly enough would do. Maybe we're attracted to what we know. Familiarity breeds familiarity. Abuse consumes self-esteem. That feeling of inadequacy killed Shirley and Kindra, and battered me.

It is said that time heals all things.

Well, not all.

And it shouldn't.

XXV

Every Emotion Requires—No; Demands—Expression

"Wren, I need another break, darling."

"Yes, I understand," she said. "I'll go check on Mom."

I smiled as she rubbed my back this time, barely touching me but leaving the sensation of empathy all the same. I felt her warmth as I had when telling about the loss of my child.

"Be right back," she said.

When she was gone, I walked down the path to the playground her mother had had constructed near the playhouse. She wanted to keep our little girl a little girl for as long as possible. I sat on the swing and put it in slow motion.

By now, it had caught me – the Thing that crawls like fog beneath the rain. It changes its name often to confuse me. Today it was sadness. Last night it had been anger – at myself, at the companion I should have who refuses to show up in my life; at everyone around me who is full of words but no deeds that might adjust my circumstance in any useful way. Telling my stories gave entry to this Thing that now sat with me like a shadow. I wanted to pretend that it was some ghost wanting my attention, but this energy belonged to me. This had been my concern; that telling Wren these stories would open my soul, allowing this Thing to feed.

Yesterday its name was fear – that I had gotten it all wrong— my life—and time was calling my hand. Despite my abilities, my knowledge and the confidence I present, I am still human, working through my human stuff.

Today, it came as sadness. Fingers starved of touch touched me. Arms needing the safety of a mother's embrace strained from waiting. My eyes blinked and burned as they looked past the horizon. Left unnourished, the golden hues of my skin were tarnished with patches of dry.

The Thing came as sadness for all the *nothings* I spoke when *something* was very wrong. For the story of abuse I just shared with a child that I had never told anyone else. Sadness that the love shown me was wrapped in a crumpled paper bag from the grocery store. No bow, no sentiments, only excuses that bound it tightly at the neck. Sadness that the love I wanted was like a ship still out there on the ocean battered by the whispers of hope. Encouraged by tattered flattery pretending it's not a mirage.

Sadness that the brisk steps I took into my life were now a slow shuffle to the finish line upon feet that could walk past daffodils as if they did not matter. Clouded eyes blinked back the hurt from squinting as they followed newborn sparrows on their maiden quest across the sky to liberty.

I sat still as sadness clutched my heart until it shrank from the weight of pity. I felt the burden of regret and shame for the neglect of my own happiness.

I sat still, needing acceptance to arrive. There was no kicking or screaming. No protestation, no running, no bartering. Not even grief. I simply sat still as sadness came.

XXVI

God Is

Wren returned with two bowls of chocolate ice cream just beginning to melt.

"Mama thought you could use this," she said, handing one to me.

"Your mom has always known what I needed. Chocolate is my favorite."

Wren took the swing next to me. She had changed into her favorite blue jeans and a yellow sweater. She'd replaced her sandals with yellow and green plaid tennis shoes. The green specks in her eyes shined against her bronze skin. Her ponytail had gone from one to two that hung over her ears and brushed her shoulders. Everyone ooed over the little girl with the buoyant silver hair, asking how that could be. Truth was, her great grandmother, Nola, had a wide streak of silver from the time she was five. But I'd tell them, "She's an old soul who chose to keep her beautiful gray hair." I imagined it was the same with grandma Alice and her legs.

After a few broad licks on her spoon she said, "Tell me about church, Gaia. Why do you go?"

"Ohhhh..". A smile crossed my face as I closed my eyes for a second. "Why... do... I... go... to... church... I opened my eyes and looked out into nature. "I go now for the memories."

I loved church as a kid. It was Grandma Alice's favorite place. Most go to church to praise God, some go to be seen. I went for the entertainment. The stories were as exciting as my Greek and Roman mythologies. The music pleased my soul and the shouters never disappointed. Some stories were problematic though. For example, the angry, destroyer God was troublesome. Any devastation or burden in our family or community was accepted as God's will. I couldn't reconcile that with the God who dusted the night with stars to light our way, flowers of every color and perfume to beautify the day, an assortment of birds to harmonize the air; trees that fed different forms of life and shaded us from heat, water that came as rain, sleet and snow to sustain these creations. Could that God willfully inflict pain and suffering? Confused and curious, I went to Mr. Cecil.

He smiled. After a while, he said, "If God doesn't do over, neither does anything stay the same. As the Universe expands and we grow in knowledge, what looks like destruction could be evolution. It's the same as you bursting the seam of a dress that no longer fits. You get a new one, right?"

"Okay. So what is God?" I asked.

"Close your eyes," he said. "Put your hands over your ears and tell me what you hear and see." It was a quiet day and I covered my ears well. After a moment or so I said, "Nothing."

I felt him close to my head. "Yes," he said; "Exactly. That is God. Now open your eyes and ears." I did so. "Tell me what you see and hear."

I named everything I could see and hear, even my little buddies making their way with the carcass of an unfortunate beetle.

"That is God," he said.

"Doesn't God live in church? They call it the Lord's house."

He put my hand over my heart. "Do you feel your heartbeat?"

"Yes," I said, and promptly asked , "Is God my heartbeat?"

He smiled. "Noo... God lives between the beats. That building is simply a place where so-called believers conduct rituals to praise their idea of God, but often end up praising themselves."

This was heavy stuff for a ten year old offered a steady diet of hellfire and damnation administered by a God who sat high and punished for spitting on the grass on Sunday.

I got up, ending the lesson with my hand still over my heart, feeling its tha-thump tha-thump. I went to my favorite place, the cemetery, to think about what Mr. Cecil had said. I looked at everything and listened to every sound around me. Everything I saw and heard was simply being what it was. This was church! In the very act of being, everything was expressing its manifestation of God right where it was. Even a scorching sun.

I smiled and said, "Hello God."

Wren licked her spoon before slowly whirling it inside the bowl to catch the melting ice-cream. "What is it sweetness," I said. "I see a question all over that gorgeous face."

She thought for a minute before asking, "How does God choose who will be born and when?"

"Oh my goodness. What a big question."

"Well?" Wren said.

"By game show, silly. Have you ever seen *The Price is Right?* Well, it's like that. Saint Peter yells out several names from a stadium full of souls: *"Come on Down, It's Time to Live Your Life!"* Then they get to play for all the great skills and talents God has behind the curtain. Some get one possession, some get several. A few, like you, hit the game-show jackpot. And the best part is, nobody gets born empty-handed."

"But aren't we all born equal?" she asked.

"Not even close."

XXVII

Adversity is Not Meant to Define, but to Reveal Who We Are

While everyone else was feeding me fear, Mr. Cecil fed me self-esteem. He opened my mind to infinite possibilities. But Grandma Alice kept us in check. She told us we were not better than anybody else; and we weren't less than anyone either. I didn't even know we were poor until some teacher labeled me so and treated me as such. I don't think she meant to discriminate because she went out of her way to be nice to me. Whatever the motive, her message was that I was *less than*. I eventually won her over because my mind was *more* than. Certainly more than she expected.

Mr. Cecil helped to neutralize that teacher's damage. He taught me to question, analyze and explore. As I think about it, I wonder how my shyness was able to incorporate his defiant concepts.

"Defiant?" Wren said, her inflection rising at the end.

Yes. Defiant. It's a marvelous word. To defy means to resist or challenge, to dare; to change. Your grandma, Alice, was like that - bold, daring, defiant. She was a living example long before I understood the word.

The opposite of defiance is obedience. More people than not are afraid to challenge the expectations of their parents, significant other, children, church, job, culture. They are shaped like clay into what others would have them be. And then shaped again by society's expectations from adulthood to death. Some people are just fine conforming because it allows them to justify sacrificing their dreams on the alter of obedience. Day after day, they cream their morning coffee with regret.

If there is one thing I hate more than anything, it's someone telling me who or what I am. I'm usually labeled after I've taken a position or demonstrated a behavior contrary to their expectation. In others words, I didn't conform. They'd say, "You're mean... you're hard... why are you so difficult..." There is no recognition that I am defiant, self-aware; no appreciation at all for that.

Growing up, I observed examples of a good wife. Television wives taught me, women in my community showed me that a good wife bends to the desires of her husband. A good wife makes meatloaf from her ambition and feds her family her dreams. She hides her intelligence behind an apron in order to boost her husband's worth. A good wife sacrifices herself for the sake of the marriage. She is even loyal beyond her husband's death when she buries her future with him.

The wives I saw on television and in my neighborhood were smarter than their husbands, and knew it; so did the husbands. But their marriages had this unspoken agreement about how needs would be met and who was in charge. Wives' needs usually went unfilled because they were perceived as having no value beyond the husband's identity. Some women clutch the scripture that tells wives to submit to their husband, without understanding what that really means. Some cheated, spent, ignored, or emasculated the husband as her compensation in this unspoken agreement. The best of these good wives knew how to manipulate her husband in a way that left his ego intact.

My mother's fear came true. I married and had Shannon while in college. I gave myself over to making a good home for my family. I accepted my husband's wandering eyes, hands, and the rest of him that followed. Somewhere in the desire to be a good wife and mother, I knew the truth of what would become of me if I gave all of me to this notion of marriage, especially this marriage. So, I didn't.

After a while, the put-downs started as if it was the most natural thing. I heard things like, 'My mom makes better biscuits' or a question like, 'Is this clean?' On the surface, they were harmless, but all I heard was *you're not good enough.*

Eventually the physical abuse began. Although he never said the words, I came to believe my husband resented me for not giving him my heart; for not complying with the unspoken agreement. He resented me for not submitting.

After nine years, culminating in the night that I told you about, I left him. For my survival and your mother's sake, I became defiant. After my journey in the tunnel, where I literally saw the light, I stopped being a piece of clay to being a piece of pottery.

I've been tempered by fire stoked with adversity, emotional and physical abuse, oppression, racism, and sexism. Rather than cracking from the heat, I became a work of beauty: strong, unique, resilient. That was fire's gift to me.

During it all, I would hear Mr. Cecil's instruction: "Don't let nobody turn you around." He said, "You can be the dust or you can be the broom. You know what I'm saying?"

I was a kid, I had no idea what he was saying but I nodded anyway. Eventually, I came to understand.

I remember sharing my hurt feelings with Mr. Cecil over one thing or another. Probably from the picking I got for being so skinny; and he said, "A reed that bends in a storm can do so because it soaks up the rain. That same reed can become a flute -- or a weapon." He took out his harmonica and played a beautiful melody that sounded like the wind doing a ballroom dance. So soft, so tender — obedient only to the notes, he played.

In the midst of our worst moments, we can become the flute and God the music that moves us through the messes we make for ourselves, the limitations others try to harness us with, or the discord when we do not live in Agreement. At those times, we must be defiant. We can't let anyone tell us who we are or who we are not. God already did and like grandma Alice said, "God didn't make no junk."

"Gaia, you do realize your stories of adversity centered around marriage, right?"

"Really? How observant; I hadn't noticed." I chuckled. "Well, all I can say to that is Gaia is a little jaded on the subject. Frankly, I don't think it should be a life-long commitment; ten years tops. When it's your turn to jump the broom, use your mom and dad as the better examples, okay?"

I looked at Wren. She had a malicious look on her face and smiled. "The other woman grandpa married felt your defiance, didn't she?"

"Yep. On that day, she was a speck of dust and I was a brand new broom."

XXVIII

You Don't Need Words to Pray

The human species is self-correcting, something like your computer resetting itself when time changes, or alerting you when it has a problem. Just as Code corrects your computer, Prayer helps us back on course. Remember: what God will do is already done. We are made to be self-sustaining. God imbued each of us with purpose, abilities to manage that purpose and the presence of others to support it. We were given everything we need to do and be what God has offered us to do and be.

But there are times when we are weary, or confused, and have forgotten who we are. So we call upon God for guidance and restoration. Prayer should be about aligning with God. But what do we pray? For God to give all, fix all. We want what we call obstacles to be removed, or our enemies to perish. Rarely do we say *thank you* to the *experience*. Rarely do we acknowledge the gifts of maturation and clarity available within those obstacles. We want to skip the unpleasantness and go straight to happily-ever-after. It's like skipping the vegetables at dinner and going straight to dessert. Those vegetables have nourishment necessary to our body as the unpalatable has to the soul. We tend to sublimate ourselves as if we are powerless, and at the mercy of every force we encounter.

Whatever the outcome, we call it God's will. But God's will is simply that we be the manifestation of God given each of us to be. The unpleasant stuff are simply decisions we've made and attitudes we've adopted waving their arms yelling "woohoo!" When it has your attention it says, "boo-boo, really?" But get this: The unpleasant has as much information, opportunity and possibility as the feel-good stuff. As you said, it's *all* good, if we let it be.

What is it to pray, then? Imagine that God is an endless river with streams that flow in all directions. No matter where you go, a stream is nearby. Imagine being a traveler on a grand quest of discovery. You've made some wrong turns, encountered some rough terrain, begun to doubt your fitness for the task. At that moment, you happen upon a stream. You sit down beside the water and take a sip. You take off your shoes and let your toes play in the coolness. That stream is the source of all we need to replenish us, to restore our faith. We never ask the stream to refresh us, or nourish, or cool us; these are in the nature of the river. So why ask the river to do what the river does? Likewise, why ask God to do what God has already done or give what you already have? You change a situation by *changing* the situation.

So, what is it to pray? Think of it as resting in that gently flowing stream. But if you must use words, say, "*Thank you.*"

XXIX

God Does Not See Everything

Thank you, God!

God has given us unlimited authority to make decisions and act according to our sense of self, our relationship with others, our belief systems, and our faith. Why would God care what I had for lunch or what movie I saw Sunday night? God does not sit in the window watching like a neighbor on the block.

"But what about Judgment Day," Wren asked.

With every gift and possession, God has given us the grace to screw up. Humans — because we are curious, defiant, doubtful, ignorant; revengeful, emotional, compliant, and everything else — make mistakes. We all step outside our frequency at some point. Thankfully, I believe God loves us just the same.

The story that God sees everything is a way to force ourselves and each other into some preferred behavior. When the outcome falls short, we say God jots it down in some big book to be judged when we die. I believe we were given a moral compass built in. In the grand scheme of things, we know what is right from not right, fair from unfair; just from unjust. Like the computer informs the user, that compass tells us when we're not following God's intent.

Being a parent, son or daughter, sister or brother, can be the hardest duty on earth to fulfill. No matter how we try, we don't always get it right. On the rare occasion that we live up to the expectation, there is no accolade because getting it right is expected. Even God gets admonished for too much rain or not enough.

Sweetheart, each of us wants to be loved; to know that we matter; that what we do is favorably acknowledged, that what we give is gratefully received. If you've done all that you can do, be satisfied with your efforts, even if others are not. Your best effort, at that moment, is all that God requires.

Even so, we must recognize that people are not at the same place emotionally, physically, materially, or spiritually. No one else can do what you do. In these ways, we are not equal. We must extend the rope of patience; set the table with a bottle of grace. If we keep trying to be the best mother or father, sister or brother, daughter or son, friend, or neighbor, let that be enough. With patience and grace, one day we might arrive at the place we are expected.

Likewise, God invites us to get it right, to stay in our frequency, to follow our moral compass, and supports our efforts with grace and patience. If we accept free will, we must acknowledge that possibility. And if we accept that we must accept our best is good enough.

XXX

We Are Not Alone

"Gaia, If God has done everything, and doesn't see everything, and we don't need words to pray, how do miracles happen?"

"Good question!" I said.

I picked up a stick and drew four lines in the dirt and pointed to the last line. This line represents the physical world. Here, human beings, all other life, and manifested ideas exist. Everything in the physical world is here to serve each other. Even animals, nature and things have power to influence our lives. Our deeds can be miracles for the recipient. Ask a person who hasn't eaten in days what a meal means to him. Humans bless each other every day.

"What about animals and things?" Wren asked.

"Well, it is proven that animals can save lives, literally. Simply touching them can calm us. Seeing one abused raises our instinct to nurture or protect. I can't watch one play and not smile.

"*Things* can be blessings because they come from Higher Mind. Television, airplanes and the computer still amaze me. Every *thing* — from the first sharpened stick, through the industrial to the technological revolution are miracles. Medicine, electricity, cell phones, the internet: all miracles."

"Okay, I get it," Wren said. "So, what is the third line?"

This line, pointing to the third mark, is where all departed life exist. They can communicate with us but can not intervene because they have not yet reached full enlightenment. They come in our dreams, talk to our hearts, give us clues they are with us. In these ways, they help guide us from their level of awareness.

The second line is the realm of Spirit. Lots of energies exist here, but the most important ones, relative to your question, are Angels. God has given them authority to intercede on behalf of everything in the physical realm. We don't often recognize these interventions because we see them as minor events; it's the big ones that get our attention. We praise God for missing a flight that crashed minutes later, or finding someone alive after days in a conceivably fatal circumstance. But we dismiss a friend coming along with just the words we need to hear. Angels don't rate what they do.

I tapped the top line. This represents God. I used the stick to draw a circle connecting all the lines and drew a line through the circle down the middle like the mathematical zero. All is God.

I looked at Wren. "Do you understand, Precious?"

"I do," she answered. "That is the basis of that unconditionally loving, co-evolving eco-system orbiting within a constellation of events where help is always nearby. Amazing," she said.

"Who you telling?!"

XXXI

Everything is Holy – But Most of All: Time

Some say that God lives in us and all living things. Others say that God resides in Heaven. For others, God is the Energy that binds the Universe. What I believe for certain is that we understand God through our relationships with each other and every living thing. Through every emotion, as a result of every decision, in every belief we have about ourselves. This makes *everything* holy.

"I thought holy means something is infused with God's energy," Wren said, "like the Grail in the Indiana Jones movies."

Exactly! But most people think holy means to walk around in righteousness—whatever that means. That holy means perfect—whatever that means. They apply the word so narrowly that they deny and oppress who they are and judge others unworthy of God's grace. Then they call their own conjured behavior moral. They fail to see *everything* is holy, even that which they judge.

Biblical scholars say that holy means *set apart*. Usually from the world, from emotions, from our own thoughts. But why would God ask us to separate from the world when the world is God's creation? Do we really want to be apart from other manifested thoughts of God? How is that possible anyway? These scholars usually mean we should set ourselves apart from that part of our culture, other people, our thoughts, desires and emotions that they call evil. But the things they want to set us apart from inform who we are. Ask anyone who has tried to deny any aspect of their nature and they'll tell you it's agony; some say it's hell.

Out of this fanatical thinking, some say humans are born in sin and are therefore sinful. But here's a concept. Think of holy as *aligned with* rather than set apart from. Now, hold that thought. I need to deviate.

Time is space, and space is time – but neither really exists, right?

"Right," Wren answered. "Both measure the distance between points."

Riiight. Between now and then is space and time. Between here and there is space and time. Between you and me is space and time. In that space and time is God. I talked about this earlier with the heartbeat example. But I want to talk about time in a different way.

The first *thing* God designated as holy in the Christian Bible is a day. Genesis 2:2-3 says:

> "By the seventh day God had finished the work He had been
>   doing; so on the seventh day He rested from all His work.
>   And God blessed the seventh day and made it holy, because on
>   it He rested from all the work of creating that He had done."

God rested. What God will do was done. When do we rest? Usually when the job is finished. However, before completion, God is said to have stepped back and examined the progress, and called it Good. But reviewing is not 'resting'. When finished, God had made everything, infused *with* God's energy. Therefore: Holy.

As we said, a day is simply a measure of time and space. In recognition of God sanctifying the seventh day—however long or short that was—as holy, humankind was instructed to set aside the sabat; which means a unique time to stop, to rest. "Remember the Sabbath and keep it holy" is a command to be still and know God, to reflect upon that which is finished, both of God's creations and our own.

We are asked to stop, from time to time, and observe the holiness of space between one thing and another. That time and space can be a second, as we know it, or a thousand years. So, when you see someone who appears to be doing nothing, don't judge; he or she could be in sabat. The Buddha sat, some say, for forty days contemplating God. Moses wandered for forty years before receiving divine awareness.

Now, back to the concept of holy as 'aligned with'. Here's an example. Consider two magnets. Apart, they are separate polarities. Nothing happens when things are set apart. But put them in proximity and an intangible energy stream draws them to each other. They become aligned. They become more of what they are.

When two people argue, they set themselves apart; they move out of their frequency with each other. But God is still in the space between.

When we are aligned, the relationship expands the capacity of each person. They becomes more. The relationship takes on its own identity and substance. Poets have written about such relationships for centuries. *That* energy is God. That relationship is *holy*. It does not mean the relationship is without challenges; it means they honor the challenges with respect and adoration.

So why are some relationships disastrous? Because one does not honor the other. Because the two are not of like energy, on opposing wavelengths. Being equal doesn't mean being the same, doing the same or having the same. It means being of compatible frequencies at the soul level. It means respecting the abilities and skills of the other. They are equal in how they value the relationship. Some energies are toxic in the presence of the other. Like Clorox and ammonia, they shouldn't mix. These relationships can be detrimental to each, those around them and even to life itself.

More than anything, we fail to accept that all things begin and end. We tend to hold on long after the relationship has served its purpose. Transitions can be painful; we might even suffer. But suffering has value. It allows us to release, to empty, to adjust the fantasy we might have had. We shouldn't demonize the relationship, but acknowledge it with gratitude. No doubt, it has restored a memory of who we are, or are not.

Secondly. We revere time. We long for time past, hope for time future and party in the present. We are devoted to and worship time. We even try to make more time and call it multitasking. We've created all kinds of luxuries to free ourselves from the confines of time but then fill that freedom with more *doing*. In all our doing, we forget the sabat. We forget to pause. We forget to reflect, to breath, to let go and restore. We forget to pray. The question becomes: do we worship time from a place of rest to align with God, or as a commodity for more doing?

"God made the end of each day a sabat, Gaia, because we sleep," Wren added. "And some people talk to God at bedtime in an effort to stay connected."

Not only that, Wren, when we 'pause' to watch a sunset, or play with a pet, we smile. Our biology and physiology are positively affected. People are said to live longer when they stop doing and spend affirming time in the presence of something being. So even during the day, we can be in sabat.

When we stop to think about how our actions affect another, God is in the space between the thought and the response. Sometimes our first reaction to an unpleasant situation is to retaliate; if not then, later. But with time to compose, with God in the space, we might decide to let it be. Likewise, a decisive response is the right course of action if it brings things back into alignment.

Time is void until we fill the space with energy. Time becomes intelligent, reflective, creative, or destructive. It becomes measured. We came into being at a particular time and will cease at a moment in time. I'm paraphrasing Ecclesiastes 3, but it is said, "To everything there is a season, and a time to every purpose under the sun..." A time to plant and a time to pluck that which is planted, a time to laugh, cry, mourn, to dance, a time to fight, embrace, get, lose, keep; a time to speak, to keep silent; there's even a time to kill.

Time is a gift made holy so that we might know God. Time is the gift that allows us to question our own actions, to examine our own works, to measure our own deeds. Time is the unique gift we give each other to be, and do, and become – or overcome.

Time is holy when it brings us into alignment with God, and each other. Within the construct of time, everything happens.

XXXII

And We Begin Again

This was my Truth to Wren. It was not the whole truth but as much as I could tell her for now. She bent and picked up a pebble that she tossed into the stream. The plop of it breaking the water's flow caused a bird to take flight. The trees surrounding us held the August heat at bay. A soft breeze rustled the leaves to help move the evening air.

"That's enough for now, Gaia," Wren said. "You've given me lots to think about. I have to figure out what it all means."

"What is this about, baby girl?"

Wren hesitated. "A woman appeared in my dream last night. She said, 'Prepare to meet the King of Peace'. She said to know him, I must know the ways of God."

"Did she say why?" The Mothers had told me this day would come but I wanted to know what Wren was asked to do.

"I think I have to confront this King of Peace, and you have information that will help me face him. She cautioned that only the Mothers—and you—are equipped to teach me since I have not yet had the pleasure of understanding God personally. I get it; I'm just now ten years old. How much can I know?" Wren smiled.

I knew what she meant; I've been concerned with her readiness to face the man who calls himself the King of Peace, at whatever age, since her birth. His nature was unsettling, but Wren was born for this. Her mother and I are a part of her mission, so she will not face him alone. Her cousin Malice has spent years preparing for this encounter.

"Do you know who he is, Gaia, this King of Peace? Is it God? And why do I have to confront him?"

"No. Baby. He is a man, but more than a man. Mechisedec is the name he gave himself. He is the most unique individual science has ever created."

"He was created by science?" Curiosity rode her voice.

"The doctor who attended to you and your mother when she was shot experimented on him when he was a child. That little boy was an orphan and not the doctor's only subject. But he developed in ways science could not predict. I'll call Malice; he'll fill you in about that. Those experiments changed him. Of all the things he might have become, he became a killer. A judge was the last person, we believe, to die at his hands. He cut off people's hands and feet and nailed them to crosses, leaving short prayers with each body.

"I see," Wren said. "You said he *chose* the name Mechisedec. It must mean something to him."

"The original Mechisedec was a king who existed before Jesus was born. The name means priest of the most high God. Abraham blessed this king and gave him what might have been the first tithe of ten percent of all he had. Mechisedec is said to have been without mother, without father, having neither beginning of days or end of life. The Biblical Mechisedec has been called the king of righteousness, the king of peace."

I felt Wren's concern. "Wren, Malice believes this man killed out of vengeance. His family was poisoned with yellow jasmine."

"Yellow jasmine? It's one of the most poisonous plants on the east coast. Was he poisoned? He survived? How?"

"Baby, of all the things I've said, what resonates with you? That is what you should focus on. Truth resonates with truth."

"What's resonates with me is everything is connected; that we all have possessions that can elevate each other if we be ourselves."

"Yes. What else?"

"That I can access Higher Mind where all answers reside; that God is between every moment; in everything that is."

"That's right, baby."

Wren rubbed the colored gemstones around her wrist. "Gaia, if cousin Malice hasn't been able to catch him, what can I do?"

"One of my favorite poets wrote: 'If you aren't in over your head, how do you know how tall you are?'" Which means a challenge helps us know what we're made of."

"Who said that?" Wren asked

"T. S. Eliot; a very wise man. You should read his work. He also said 'anxiety is the handmaiden of creativity'. I hesitated. "My love, we can only taste courage when we swallow fear."

"He said that, too?" she asked.

"No, I did."

Sweetheart, the last thing we talked about was time. Time contains all possibilities, and doubt is an illusion. You have to be as certain of yourself as Mechisedec is about being the King of Peace. Now, tell me what else you heard?"

"You said we are not to judge. But if we don't judge, how do we determine right from wrong?"

"I did say that; but throughout our conversation, I've said don't judge the *doer* because Truth evolves. Everything is a manifestations of God; but it is perfectly acceptable to protect ourselves from situations for our preservation. It was once acceptable for one group to treat other groups with what can only be described as horrific brutality. But social codes change as people mature spiritually. Then, like now, our moral compass guides us; otherwise, civilization would never change. The litmus for any action is: does it advance, or diminish the recipient, the group, or society? Is it done out of love or something else?

Besides, we don't know what you're asked to do. I do know each of us is called upon to Support, Protect, Nurture and Elevate. So, let's believe in that."

"You're right Gaia. I shouldn't assume my life is at risk. But what if what I do diminishes Mechisedec?"

"What if what you do helps Mechisedec realign with God?" I offered. "What if he can then use his possessions to advance others?"

Fear and doubt made destruction a possibility, but I could see her now processing an alternate fate than she imagined. Besides, the science of him had to intrigue her.

"Sweetness, we talked about totems and how families select symbols, or name their children to imbue them with a particular spirit or energy meant to guide the child or represent the family. Well, have you thought about why you were named Wren?"

"No, please tell me," she answered with delight.

"Well, most wrens are small and inconspicuous. Unlike you with those eyes and hair." I flicked a silver ponytail off one shoulder. "The wren is a secretive bird and exceptionally smart. Its song is complex and considered pleasant to the ear.

"A German fable is told that there was a race between the birds to see who was best. The bird who could fly the highest would be made king. The eagle began stepping high with his chest full of confidence. He just knew he would be king because he could already out-fly all the other birds.

"But guess what. A tiny bird hid in the eagle's feathers! When the eagle had gone as far as he could, that little bird flew out and over the eagle's head. It was the wren! He was given a yellow crown and named kuningilin. It means cunning king of the birds. The Dutch call him winterkoninkje."

"I like that story, Gaia."

"You, my little Wren are small, your voice is charming, you're cunning and powerful, with your own silver crown."

I reached for my granddaughter and held her close. "I know this for sure: the King of Peace is no match for winterkoninkje."

We both laughed. Whatever God whispered to her to do, today it began. How it would unfold, neither of us knew. We sat quietly in prayer, in the void of Time, listening to the leaves rustle, the water gently trickle over rock, and the cadence of a bird that called from the tree above.

"Sweetheart, here's what I know: no matter our choices; in the belly of despair, or the heart of bliss; we are not alone. Ever."

 C3

About Me ~

Previous novels:

The Scent of Gardenia - *2009*

Blood of Their Sons - *2011*

I believe all events, all life are connected through intersecting threads. Much like a diagrammed sentence. Like the streams that form a river, my novels each share something in common with the other.

I believe we co-create through our relationships with God and each other to produce our experiences. I write about the choices and consequences inherent in those experiences.

I invite you to consider the ideas I've presented, whether you agree with or not. I encourage you to discuss the material with others with the hope that whatever you believe will be expanded. Sharing your truth matters.

I reside in Charlotte, NC and welcome opportunities to explore my work with groups in person, by conference call or online.

Reach me at: frogshairpress@gmail.com

Blood of Their Sons

A baby boy is close to birth. The dying matriarch of the St.John family tells a secret that ends with a certain truth: that child must not come into the world. As far back as their history is known, girls are born first. This legacy has given these first-born women abilities that must continue through time, advancing with each generation. Grace, the baby's grandmother, rejects the matriarch's dying declaration and sets out to defy the St.John legacy. Her goal is to defend her daughter's child; but she meets destiny in her efforts to save him.

ෆ

The Scent of Gardenia

In the aftermath of Hurricane Floyd, a casket containing the body of a white woman is discovered coursing through Princeville, an eastern North Carolina town. She's been secretly buried in a black cemetery thirty years before. Several states away, a serial killer is cutting off hands and feet, nailing them to a cross. A federal agency with secrets of its own has discovered he is one of their creations. They later learn he is linked to the white woman's death. How is that possible; she died before their creation was born?

I
N
D
E
X

163

♋

When we have let go of *everything*;
When we have glimpsed ourselves in each other,
When we have given birth to our imaginations,
We will know God.

~ mebs

www.ingramcontent.com/pod-product-compliance
Lightning Source LLC
Chambersburg PA
CBHW051042030426
42339CB00006B/148